Making Tax Sense

To my brother Dennis —
Thank you for all of your
help on this.

Kevin

Making Tax Sense

The Case for a Progressive Consumed-Income Tax

M. Kevin McGee

LEXINGTON BOOKS
Lanham • Boulder • New York • London

Published by Lexington Books
An imprint of The Rowman & Littlefield Publishing Group, Inc.
4501 Forbes Boulevard, Suite 200, Lanham, Maryland 20706
www.rowman.com

6 Tinworth Street, London SE11 5AL, United Kingdom

British Library Cataloguing in Publication Information Available

Library of Congress Cataloging-in-Publication Data

Names: McGee, M. Kevin, 1958- author.
Title: Making tax sense : the case for a progressive consumed-income tax / M.
   Kevin McGee.
Description: Lanham : Lexington Books, [2019] | Includes bibliographical
   references and index.
Identifiers: LCCN 2018060931 (print) | LCCN 2019000464 (ebook) | ISBN
   9781498587181 (electronic) | ISBN 9781498587174 (cloth : alk. paper)
Subjects: LCSH: Income tax—United States. | Tax expenditures—United States.
   | Taxation—United States.
Classification: LCC HJ4652 (ebook) | LCC HJ4652 .M3874 2019 (print) | DDC
   336.240973—dc23
LC record available at https://lccn.loc.gov/2018060931

∞™ The paper used in this publication meets the minimum requirements of
American National Standard for Information Sciences—Permanence of Paper
for Printed Library Materials, ANSI/NISO Z39.48-1992.

Printed in the United States of America

Contents

List of Tables

Chapter One

The Problem

As we all know, the current Federal income tax system is a mess. It's enormously complicated. It's loaded with special provisions of questionable value. And it's rife with inconsistencies that are regularly used to create tax shelters. On the day you file your tax return, do you ever feel sure that what you've filed is totally and exactly accurate? Have you gotten all of the tax breaks coming to you, neither too few nor too many? Or do you usually, after spending as much time as you can possibly stand to spend with the forms or the tax software or the tax pro you've hired, finally throw up your hands and say OK, good enough, I sure hope this goes through?

The sentiment is pretty much unanimous, on both sides of any political aisle: our income tax system needs fixed.[1] It needs either dramatically repaired, or replaced somehow, but what repairs, or what do we replace it with? What fix would actually make sense?

If you ask a Republican what the fundamental flaw in our tax system is, you'll probably be told about how it affects incentives, especially the incentives to save and invest.[2] If you ask a Democrat what's the fundamental flaw in our tax system, you'll probably hear about its loopholes, which the well-off use to avoid paying their fair share of taxes.[3] In a sense both are correct—those are indeed problems with our current tax system, problems that might seem to be polar opposites, since the Republicans' fixes for their perceived problem usually makes the Democrats' perceived problem worse, and vice versa.

But really, they're both wrong. For, while these are indeed problems with our current tax system, they are not the fundamental problem, but only symptoms of that problem. Rather, the fundamental flaw in our tax system is that it is *incoherent*, in the sense of being disjointed, or disconnected. A well-designed tax system is like a good jigsaw puzzle: all the pieces fit together

1

snugly, and when the whole thing is fully assembled, it forms a coherent picture that makes sense to any onlooker. In contrast, our current tax system resembles a jigsaw puzzle made up of parts of a dozen different puzzles. Some of the pieces fit with others, but there are many that have no natural place. Sandwiched between these pieces are holes and gaps that can be readily exploited by clever tax lawyers and accountants.

An incoherent tax system is necessarily inconsistent and unfair. If the various parts of the tax system aren't all based on the same design, then different types of income are taxed differently, leaving some taxpayers with a heavier tax burden than others, even on the same total income. That in turn leads to tax gamesmanship, as those who can afford tax lawyers seek ways to convert their higher-taxed income into some lower-taxed form.

An inconsistent tax system is also more complicated. Rules that demarcate one form of income from another are needed, as are regulations that push back against the more creative games that get invented. These rules result in complex formulas and calculations—like the 45-line Schedule D Tax Worksheet. And millions of taxpayers end up reading the same set of directions a third time, trying to figure out whether this particular tax treatment applies to them or not.

In addition, an inconsistent tax system distorts taxpayer incentives. If different investments get different tax treatments, investors will be prone to seek out not the most productive investments, but the ones that are most tax-favored. Our national savings is channeled into relatively low (before tax) return uses, and our economic efficiency suffers.

So how did we get this mess in the first place? The original sin, so to speak, was to try to adopt what I will call a "traditional income tax"—that is, a tax levied on all income, when that income is earned. As we will see in chapter 2, a traditional income tax includes pieces that don't quite mesh, such as taxing pensions, owner-occupied housing, and capital gains in ways that are simply not feasible. As a result, a truly coherent traditional income tax is simply not feasible.

And that in turn has opened up the door for tax lobbyists and often well-meaning politicians to make things worse. Because provision X doesn't exactly fit with provision Y, the people taxed according to Y appear to have a legitimate complaint that requires some kind of "fix"—which in turn creates issues with provision Z. As "fix" after "fix" pile up, the system becomes more illogical, less fair, more complicated, and more exploitable. And before long, you have a mess just like ours.

The solution that I will propose in this book is to abandon the goal of a traditional income tax, in favor of its close cousin, the "consumed-income tax."[4] Like its cousin, a consumed-income tax is a tax levied on all income.

The difference is one of timing: under a consumed-income tax, income is taxed not in the year that the income is earned, but rather in the year that it is consumed.[5] For most of us, for most of our income, those are one and the same: most of my earnings in 2017 were spent in 2017. As a result, for the overwhelming majority of Americans, a consumed-income tax would look and feel almost exactly like our current income tax does, albeit with a few simplifications that would make our lives just a little bit easier.

As we will see in chapter 3, consumption-timed taxes do not have the same inherent shortcomings as a traditional income tax.[6] The issues like pensions, owner-occupied housing, and capital gains that bedevil the design of a traditional income tax are handled easily and coherently once the timing changes from when-income-is-earned to when-income-is-consumed. Admittedly, consumption-timed taxes are not without their flaws, their complexities, and their complications. But all those flaws, complexities, and complications also arise with a traditional income tax. So consumption-timed taxes, while not perfect, are by their very nature much more coherent than a traditional income tax could ever hope to be.

As we will also see, switching to a consumed-income tax would address the primary complaints of Republicans and Democrats alike. A consumed-income tax treats saving and investing much more favorably than a traditional income tax, because it is built around what has become a familiar part of our tax system, the tax-deferred savings account, or IRA. Indeed, IRAs do not naturally fit into a traditional income tax, which is why contributions to IRAs, pension funds, 401(k)s, and the like are currently reported by the Federal Government as the second largest "tax expenditure'" in our tax system.[7] Under a traditional income tax, IRAs and the like look like special, preferential tax treatments that should ideally be targeted for elimination, and at minimum be severely limited.[8] In contrast, under a consumed-income tax, they make perfect sense. So switching to a consumed-income tax would allow us to broaden the use of IRAs and simplify most of the rules about them, giving almost all saving and investing very favorable tax treatment—something Republicans would broadly applaud.

Democrats might also like the consumed-income tax, because it can easily be made exactly as progressive as our current income tax.[9] The consumed-income tax would have low tax rates for those of modest means and high tax rates for those who are most well off. It would include personal and dependent exemptions that take one's family circumstances into account. It could, and in my opinion should, continue to have features like the earned income tax credit, that helps offset the impact of social security taxes on the working poor. Unlike a Flat tax or a Federal sales tax, it would not (from the Democrat's perspective) unfairly shift taxes from the rich to the poor.

So possibly, just possibly, a consumed-income tax could represent a win for both parties, and an opportunity for bipartisan reform. Indeed, it is almost certainly the only fundamental tax reform that has any chance of garnering support on both sides of the political aisle. I will explore that issue—the political possibilities of a consumed-income tax—in more detail in chapter 15, after we've identified what moving to a coherent tax system would actually involve.

In the chapters to come, we'll take a look at the big picture, at what makes a tax system work well, and what causes a system to fail. I'll then explore the various tax reform options, one choice at a time, and recommend what I believe are the best choices for us to make. My recommendations will be based on three criteria. The first, and most important, will be coherence: what option best fits with all the other choices already made; what option best leads to a sensible, coherent tax system. After all, if we want a tax system that actually makes sense, we need to make sure that every piece jibes with all the other pieces of the puzzle.

The second criterion will be simplicity. As we will see, the logic of a consumed-income tax often provides us with more than one way to achieve coherency. Unless there is a good reason to choose complexity, I will always recommend the simpler choice, the one that involves the least amount of record keeping and paperwork. Simplicity also aligns with fairness. Whenever our choice is between taxing two behaviors in the same way or in different ways, both fairness and simplicity will argue in favor of applying the same rules to everyone.

The third criterion will be minimizing change. Because our current tax system is such a mess, change is absolutely necessary. But change is disruptive, and disruption creates winners and losers (at least some of whom will then attempt to block whatever reform we propose). So if we want a proposal that has any chance of being achievable, part of our goal must be to identify the options that get us to coherence by the shortest route, with as little disruption as possible.

Among other things, minimizing change means minimizing either windfall gains or windfall losses from tax reform. As we will discuss in chapter 7, dramatic shifts in tax burdens are usually considered unfair, and are often strongly resisted even by those who are not immediately affected by the shift. No change in the tax system can entirely avoid either windfall gains or windfall losses. However, a well-designed change should try to keep them to an absolute minimum.

What we'll find by the end of the book is that true reform—involving a reasonable mix of changes that Republicans might like and changes that Democrats might favor—may actually be possible. Yes, political compromise would certainly be needed (not an easy thing given our current political polarization). But the outcome would very much make economic sense, and perhaps make political sense as well.

So this is a book about sensible *and* potentially achievable tax reform.

NOTES

1. For interesting historical summaries of how our tax system got to where it is today, written by tax experts that had front row seats, see Graetz (1997) and Steuerle (2004).

2. Republican Platform (2016).

3. Democrats.org (2016).

4. It is also sometimes called a "personal cash flow tax," or a "personal expenditure tax."

5. There are a number of different taxes that are consumption-timed. The consumed-income tax is the one this book will focus on; the others will be discussed in chapter 4. We'll discuss the issue of income not consumed before a person dies—his or her estate—in chapter 9.

6. We have a naming problem in the tax policy arena. We could call all consumption-timed taxes "consumption taxes," but that term is indelibly connected in the minds of the public and policy makers with taxes levied on sales transactions, like a sales tax—which is indeed one example of a consumption-timed tax. But there are other consumption-timed taxes, like the consumed-income tax, that are collected in exactly the same ways as our current income tax, but are based on income consumed, that is, income net of saving. To avoid getting all of these other taxes misinterpreted as sales-type taxes, I am using the somewhat inelegant term "consumption-timed taxes" for the whole tax family.

7. These contributions make up items 144, 145, 146, and 148 in the Treasury Department's report on Tax Expenditures (U.S. Treasury Department 2017). Together they added up to $194 billion in lost tax revenue in 2018, relative to a traditional income tax, second only to the $228 billion in tax revenue lost to the tax exclusion of employer-provided health insurance. Tax Expenditures will be discussed in more detail in chapter 12.

8. Henceforth, whenever I use the term "IRA" I will be referring not just to IRAs themselves, but also to all the other tax instruments, such as 401(k)s and defined-benefit pension plans, that allow savings to be put into tax deferred accounts. However, if I wish to refer to Roth IRAs, I will always specifically mention "Roth."

9. A progressive tax is any tax that imposes a higher tax rate on those with higher incomes. Because our current income tax has a series of increasing tax brackets, it is progressive. A consumed-income tax would typically also have a series of increasing tax brackets, allowing it to be equally progressive.

Chapter Two

The Impossibility of a Coherent Traditional Income Tax

The design principle behind the Traditional Income Tax is meant to be simple: tax all income when that income is earned. That sounds easy, but as it turns out, that's a very difficult principle to achieve.

The main problem involves how to measure some forms of income. Income is everything you earn, whether those earnings are used to buy the goods and services you consume, or whether those earnings are saved, adding to your net worth.[1] Most of our income, whether income from working or interest on our savings, arrives either as a check or as a deposit into a bank account. Measuring that income is easy. But some of our income comes in other, less easy to measure forms. And that creates problems.[2]

PENSIONS

Take for example the case of pensions. Suppose you're employed for a year, and part of your earnings come in the form of a future pension. You might argue that since you haven't been paid the pension yet, only promised it, this shouldn't count as income. But as I stated above, income is everything you earn, whether those earnings are used to buy the goods and services you consume, or whether those earnings are saved, adding to your net worth. And that promise of a future pension increases your net worth—so it's income.

Now, if the pension plan is of the "defined contribution" type—for example, your employer matches a part of your contributions to a 401(k)—measuring that income, by measuring the employer's match, is easy. But suppose the pension plan is of the "defined benefits" type. Then your future pension will be determined by some formula based on your years of service and other factors. As a result, calculating your increase in net worth—how much more valuable

your future pension is today than it was a year ago—is nearly impossible. So
we don't even try, leaving this income entirely untaxed until the pension benefits are actually paid out.

Yes, that's the logical way to handle these pensions. Indeed, it's the only
sensible way to handle them. But it's not consistent with the logic of a traditional income tax. And that creates problems.

One problem is fairness. Suppose I get promised a "defined benefit" pension, which won't be taxed until I retire 20 years from now. So my employer
deposits $1,000 this year into a pension reserves account. The account earns
5% a year for 20 years, building up to $2,653, which I then receive. After I
pay my income tax—let's say it's a 20% tax—I get $2,123 (table 2.1).[3]

You don't get a pension, but your employer compensates you for that by
paying you an extra $1,000 this year. You also pay a 20% income tax on this
income, and then deposit the remaining $800 into a savings account that also
earns 5% annually. After 20 years your original $1,000 will have grown to
just $1,753, 17% less than my pension—because my $1,000 wasn't counted
as income until I retired, and yours, plus the interest, was counted as income
each year (table 2.1).

Table 2.1.   The Pension Advantage

	Your Savings			*My Pension*	
Year	Balance	Interest	Tax	Pension Acct.	Tax
0	$800.00	$40.00	$8.00	$1,000.00	$0.00
1	$832.00	$41.60	$8.32	$1,050.00	$0.00
2	$865.28	$43.26	$8.65	$1,102.50	$0.00
3	$899.89	$44.99	$9.00	$1,157.63	$0.00
4	$935.88	$46.79	$9.36	$1,215.51	$0.00
5	$973.31	$48.67	$9.73	$1,276.29	$0.00
6	$1,012.25	$50.61	$10.12	$1,340.10	$0.00
7	$1,052.74	$52.64	$10.53	$1,407.11	$0.00
8	$1,094.85	$54.74	$10.95	$1,477.47	$0.00
9	$1,138.64	$56.93	$11.39	$1,551.34	$0.00
10	$1,184.18	$59.21	$11.84	$1,628.91	$0.00
11	$1,231.55	$61.58	$12.32	$1,710.36	$0.00
12	$1,280.81	$64.04	$12.81	$1,795.88	$0.00
13	$1,332.04	$66.60	$13.32	$1,885.67	$0.00
14	$1,385.32	$69.27	$13.85	$1,979.95	$0.00
15	$1,440.74	$72.04	$14.41	$2,078.95	$0.00
16	$1,498.37	$74.92	$14.98	$2,182.90	$0.00
17	$1,558.31	$77.92	$15.58	$2,292.05	$0.00
18	$1,620.65	$81.03	$16.21	$2,406.65	$0.00
19	$1,685.47	$84.27	$16.85	$2,526.98	$0.00
20	$1,752.89			$2,653.33	$530.67
Available to Spend			$1,752.89		$2,122.66

Why the difference? Notice that you had to pay $200 in taxes when you earned the $1,000, plus $8 in taxes on the first year's $40 interest, and $8.32 on the next year's interest, and so on. I eventually had to pay that same 20% tax, both on the original $1,000 and on all the interest it accumulated. But I got to delay paying those taxes, earning interest on the $200 that I got to keep but you had to surrender to the taxman. It's as if the government had given me an interest-free loan of $200 for 20 years, and then another interest-free loan of $8 for 19 years, and $8.32 for 18 years, and so on. I benefited by being able to delay paying my taxes in a way that you couldn't—which, certainly from your perspective, is just not fair.

It was because of this unfairness, this much-more-favorable tax treatment given to people who got pensions, that IRAs, 401(k)s, and other such "qualified accounts" were created—so you could have the same favorable tax treatment that I got. But because these qualified accounts violate the tax system's underlying design principle, of taxing income when it is earned, and make our tax system less coherent and less consistent with that ideal, we need to have all kinds of restrictions—who can make deposits, how much you can deposit, when you can start making withdrawals, and when you have to start making withdrawals.

The thing is, once you start bending the one fundamental rule—taxing all income when it is earned—you'll need to patch all the cracks that develop with a whole lot of other rules. And pretty soon, you have exactly the mess that is our current income tax system.

CAPITAL GAINS

A second example of the difficulty of taxing all income when it is earned involves capital gains. A capital gain is the increase in the value of an asset you own, so again it's an increase in your net worth, hence income. With a traditional income tax, all real capital gains should be taxed annually, when they occur. So, if our goal is to levy a traditional income tax, any real increase in the market value of your stocks and bonds should be listed as income on your annual form 1040.[4]

There are three problems with actually doing this. One involves inflation. Part of your portfolio's increase in market value only reflects inflation; your real income would only be the "real" (inflation adjusted) capital gain. To handle this inflation problem, Congress has sometimes allowed us to exclude a portion of our capital gain from taxation, and other times taxed those capital gains at a lower rate than other income. Both are rather crude adjustments that don't even attempt to reflect the true inflation rate. Worse yet, our current tax code gives a similarly favorable tax treatment to dividend income, which has

no inflationary component to it. And our tax code ignores entirely the inflation component in both interest income and interest payments on loans. This
wildly inconsistent treatment of inflation is patently unfair, it distorts investment decisions, and it opens the door to a variety of tax shelters.

A more difficult issue with capital gains involves liquidity. If you haven't
sold any of your investment portfolio, but we tax the capital gain when it is
earned, you may not have the cash needed to pay the tax on this gain, forcing
you to sell off some of the stock you own. To handle this problem, we don't
tax capital gains until you sell the asset, "realizing" what had before been just
a paper gain. But that again violates the logic of a traditional income tax, of
taxing all income when it is earned.

There's an even more difficult problem with taxing capital gains when they
are earned. It arises when the asset is not something frequently traded. If you
were a homeowner in 2007, during the boom in housing prices, your home's
value almost certainly increased by more than the inflation rate. Under the
logic of a traditional income tax, that real gain in net worth should have been
reported on your form 1040, as part of your 2007 income.

My guess is though, you have no idea whatsoever how much your home's
value went up that year. Having your home appraised in January of 2007,
and again in January 2008, would have given you only a rough estimate of
the increase. But having your home appraised is expensive. And again, this
paper gain would not be particularly liquid—it wouldn't provide you with the
cash to pay the tax bill, unless you sold your home. This would be a particular
problem for the elderly, many of whom are house-rich but cash-poor.

As a result, since capital gains are hard to measure for many assets and are
illiquid (not easily spent) until the assets are sold, we only tax capital gains
when they are realized, that is, when the asset that increased in value is in
fact sold. But this means that investors in capital-gains-types of assets face
a substantially lower effective tax rate than other investors. Table 2.2 shows
two investments, each earning a 10% rate of return. The first investment—a
savings account, bond fund, or money market account—earns 10% interest
income. The second—perhaps a stock fund—pays no interest, but increases
in value by 10% each year, hence generating capital gains.[5]

Notice how the story is essentially the same as what we saw in table 2.1
With the interest-earning investment, $20 of the $100 in interest earned in
year two must be paid in taxes, leaving only a balance of $1,080 to earn the
10% return in year three. With the capital gain-earning investment however,
no taxes are owed in year two, so the investor is able to earn a 10% return
on a slightly higher balance of $1,100. Once again, it is as if the capital gain
investor has been given an 18 year interest-free loan of $20 in year two, and
a 17 year interest-free loan of $21.60 in year three, and so on.[6]

Table 2.2.   Two Investments: 20 Year Comparison

Year	Interest-Earning Investment			Capital Gain Investment	
	Balance	Interest	Tax	Asset Value	Tax
1	$1,000.00			$1,000.00	$0.00
2	$1,080.00	$100.00	$20.00	$1,100.00	$0.00
3	$1,166.40	$108.00	$21.60	$1,210.00	$0.00
4	$1,259.71	$116.64	$23.33	$1,331.00	$0.00
5	$1,360.49	$125.97	$25.19	$1,464.10	$0.00
6	$1,469.33	$136.05	$27.21	$1,610.51	$0.00
7	$1,586.87	$146.93	$29.39	$1,771.56	$0.00
8	$1,713.82	$158.69	$31.74	$1,948.72	$0.00
9	$1,850.92	$171.38	$34.28	$2,143.59	$0.00
10	$1,998.99	$185.09	$37.02	$2,357.95	$0.00
11	$2,158.91	$199.90	$39.98	$2,593.75	$0.00
12	$2,331.62	$215.89	$43.18	$2,853.13	$0.00
13	$2,518.15	$233.16	$46.63	$3,138.44	$0.00
14	$2,719.61	$251.82	$50.36	$3,452.28	$0.00
15	$2,937.18	$271.96	$54.39	$3,797.51	$0.00
16	$3,172.16	$293.72	$58.74	$4,177.26	$0.00
17	$3,425.94	$317.22	$63.44	$4,594.99	$0.00
18	$3,700.01	$342.59	$68.52	$5,054.49	$0.00
19	$3,996.01	$370.00	$74.00	$5,559.94	$0.00
20	$4,315.69	$399.60	$79.92	$6,115.93	$1,023.19
Available to Spend			$4,315.69		$5,092.74

So our current income tax treats capital gains-earning investments far more favorably than other types of investments. Because we cannot consistently apply the traditional income tax design principle of taxing all income when it is earned, we end up with unfairness, and complexity, and a tax system that distorts investment incentives.

We've now seen two cases where taxing income after a delay effectively taxes that income at a lower rate: (1) a pension that is taxed eventually rather than immediately while it is earned, and (2) a capital gain that is taxed only after it's realized rather than as it builds up. Both involve income from saving and investing. Now, maybe you think that a lower tax rate on saving/investment is a good thing, and maybe you don't. But it's hard to justify a lower tax rate for some forms of saving/investing, and a higher tax rate on all other forms of saving/investing. But that's what we have, and will necessarily continue to have, with our impossible-to-exactly-implement traditional income tax.

The other way investors benefit from the "tax when realized" treatment of capital gains is by choosing what gains or losses to realize. As we've seen, if my shares have increased in value, I can reduce my effective tax rate by holding on to those shares for a long time, delaying when I pay the tax on that gain. However, if my shares have dropped in value, I have a capital loss, which under a traditional income tax is deductible. To get as much benefit from the deduction as possible, I want to realize that loss immediately.[7]

This strategy—realize losses now, hold on to gains until later—can be manipulated into a tax avoidance scheme. Suppose I invest in a pair of assets that are likely to behave as opposites, like shares in an oil company that sells oil, and shares in a chemical company that buys oil. If the price of oil goes up, my oil shares gain and my chemical shares drop. If oil prices fall, the opposite happens. Either way, I have a gain to hold on to, and a loss to realize right away. This again gives me an immediate tax deduction and only an eventual tax bill, so I can push some taxes that I would otherwise owe off into the future, and once again get in effect an interest free loan from the government.

Once again, because it's not quite possible to actually implement a traditional income tax, we end up with strategies for tax avoidance. So to limit those strategies, we load the tax code with rules—limits on the amount of losses that can be deducted each year, rules on tax straddles (opposite pairs), rules on repurchasing a stock after selling it at a loss, and so on. A lot of the tax complexity that everyone complains about exists exactly because a coherent traditional income tax in an impossible dream.

INTEREST DEDUCTIONS

Under a traditional income tax, interest income is taxed and interest payments are tax deductible. Otherwise, borrowing has no effect on tax liabilities. When the income tax was first created, the logic behind the deduction of interest payments was simple. Borrowing was something businesses did: the farmer to buy seed for this season's crop, the grocer to stock the shelves, the steamboat captain to pay for his boat. The interest paid on the loan was the cost of hiring the needed funds, no different from the wages paid to hire workers. So it made sense under a traditional income tax for interest payments to be deductible.

In our modern world of easy consumer credit, it is less obvious that the interest deduction makes sense. But that is not the real problem. The real issue is the existence of tax-deferred pension plans, and tax-only-on-realization capital gains. Because our current tax treatments of pension plans and capital gains are inconsistent with a traditional income tax, they are also inconsistent with our current tax treatment of debt. And having both sets of rules in the same tax code opens up the door for a wide variety of tax shelters.[8]

As we've seen in the above examples, any scheme that allows me to delay paying taxes for a few years will effectively reduce the tax rate I pay. If I have a $4 million capital gain, let's say on a $5 million stock portfolio, and can delay realizing the capital gain for another 10 years, my effective tax rate falls. But what if I need some of the money locked up in that stock portfolio now? Perhaps I can use the stock portfolio as collateral on a $2 million loan. I can spend most of the $2 million now, holding back some of it to pay the interest on the loan. Since the loan is fully collateralized, I'll pay a low interest rate that after taxes will be even lower, since the interest is tax deductible. Meanwhile, I'm earning a nice return on the stock portfolio, including the stock that I would have had to sell to pay the capital gains tax that I've successfully delayed—so I've created a tax shelter.

Or how about this tax shelter idea? I have a $5 million share of a real estate partnership, $2.5 million of which involves capital gains. I want to get out of the real estate investment, but don't want to realize my gains. So I have the partnership take out a $5 million loan—again using the real estate as collateral. The loan proceeds are then put into a subsidiary partnership that purchases some other assets, maybe stocks or corporate bonds. The partnership is then split up, with me getting the subsidiary with the stocks and bonds, and the other partners keeping the real estate and the loan. I now own a "partnership" invested just in stocks and bonds, instead of real estate, but I will not owe any capital gains taxes until I withdraw funds from this "partnership."

If the rest of our income tax adhered to the traditional income tax ideal, continuing our current tax treatment of debt would make perfect sense. But once we discover that that traditional ideal is impossible, borrowing becomes a vehicle to abuse the system. So again we create rules. Mortgage interest is deductible, credit card interest is not. Other interest is deductible only if it partly offsets other investment income (the IRS has a fairly complex set of "tracking rules"). As before, tax complexity results from the impossible traditional income tax dream.

INFLATION AGAIN

The problem of inflation came up before, when we discussed capital gains. But the problem of inflation affects all forms of savings income and borrowing costs under a traditional income tax.[9] Ideally, a traditional income tax is only levied on "real" income; in practice, it is invariably levied on nominal income. Suppose for example that you lent me $1,000 today, with my promise to pay you $2,100 next year. That sounds exorbitant, doesn't it—a 110% interest rate? But if we expected prices to double between now and next year (i.e., 100% inflation), that $2,100 repayment would only allow you to buy next year what you could purchase for $1,050 today. So in reality, you're only getting a 5% return on your loan.

The 110% rate is called the nominal interest rate. That's the rate that your bank posts on your credit card statement, or the rate you get quoted in all those annoying ads you receive. The 5% rate is called the real interest rate— the rate after we've taken account the impact of inflation. Roughly speaking, the real interest rate is the nominal interest rate minus the inflation rate, so if you're paying 5% nominal interest on your mortgage, but there's 2% inflation, your real interest rate is 3% (5%–2%).[10]

Technically, under the traditional income tax ideal, you should only be taxed on the 5% real return you're getting on the loan you made, and I should only be allowed to deduct the 5% real interest rate I'm paying on that loan. In actual practice though, you would be greatly overtaxed, having to pay taxes on the full 110% nominal return, and I would be over-rewarded, getting to deduct the entire 110% nominal interest rate. Perhaps calculating and reporting only the real interest rates would not be all that hard, but Congress has never felt that way. So apparently, once again levying an ideal traditional income tax is just not possible.

OWNER-OCCUPIED HOUSING

Another challenge to levying a traditional income tax involves home ownership. Suppose you bought an asset—say, an ownership share in a restaurant— and because of that investment you earned a stream of consumption—say, one free meal per week at that restaurant. Under the logic of a traditional income tax, that consumption stream should count as income, and be taxed. But when the asset that you buy is a house, you get a similar consumption stream—the shelter the house provides you. That consumption stream's market value is the rent you'd have to pay to live there, if someone else were the owner. Economists call this "imputed rent." Under the logic of a traditional income tax, since imputed rent is consumption, it should be reported annually on your form 1040, and taxed.[11]

Again however, we have a major measurement problem. What is the market rent for your home? What was it five years ago, and what will it be next year? You could hire a realtor to come in and annually give you an estimate, but again that would be cumbersome and costly. So our tax code ignores imputed rent, thereby once again falling short of a traditional income tax. And that in turn creates a variety of economic distortions—an issue we will explore in more detail in chapter 6.

THE POLITICS OF A TRADITIONAL INCOME TAX

Besides all of these measurement problems, the traditional income tax has one other glaring shortcoming—its political instability. As we will see in chapters 5 and 8, the return to savings and investing can be broken into five different components, some of which constitute what economists call the "normal" return. Taxing income when it is earned necessarily implies that we tax this normal return, which means a traditional income tax necessarily reduces the incentive to save and invest. Since the overwhelming majority of investment income is earned by high-income households, increasing the incentive to save and invest under a traditional income tax necessarily means taxing the wealthy less.

That has led to a political tug-of-war over the last half century, with Republicans reducing tax rates on investment income to improve those incentives to save and invest, and Democrats raising tax rates on investment income to improve tax progressivity. Under a traditional income tax, the two parties' goals are diametrically opposed, and each time one of them gains sufficient political power (in 1981 and 2001 and 2017 for the Republicans, and 1993 and 2013 for the Democrats), our tax system changes sharply as a result. That has resulted in, and almost certainly will continue to result in, a continual policy see-saw of repeated tax rate ups and downs, as long as we attempt to base our tax system on the ideal of a traditional income tax.

All of these problems naturally arise when we try to levy a traditional income tax. Interestingly, they either disappear entirely or are easily addressed if we merely change our target. With a traditional income tax, these problems are mostly insurmountable. But if our goal becomes levying a consumption-timed tax, these problems quickly disappear. We will turn to look at why that is.

NOTES

1. This is called the Schanz-Haig-Simons definition of income, widely accepted by economists of all political persuasions. See, e.g., Stiglitz (2000, 616), Rosen and Gayer (2010, 382), or Seidman (2009, 207). All of these references—or pretty much any other Public Finance textbook you may be able to find—provide succinct discussions of many of the issues addressed in this chapter.

2. See Bradford (1980) for a more detailed discussion of these and other similar income measurement issues.

3. Throughout the book, I will present a number of tables, illustrating some feature of either our existing or the proposed tax system. In those illustrations, I will typically be presenting flat tax scenarios—e.g., all income is taxed at a 20% rate. Those flat

rate scenarios are used to simplify the illustrations; they should not be interpreted as advocating a flat rate tax system

4. Some people—not economists—argue that capital gains are not income. So let me remind you of the Schanz-Haig-Simons definition of income that is widely used by economists: income is everything you earn, whether used to finance consumption, or saved, adding to your net worth. Capital gains add to your net worth, so capital gains are income.

5. McCaffery (2005) notes the importance of this provision in what he calls the "buy, borrow, and die" tax avoidance scheme. Wealthy individuals, by "buying capital-appreciating assets, borrowing against them to finance present consumption needs, and dying with both assets and debt in tow, . . . can avoid all federal taxation." Since the gains in this scheme were never realized, they were never taxed. Compounding the problem is that under current law the next generation, when they inherit the appreciated assets, will owe no taxes on those capital gains, due to the "stepped up basis" provision. I will discuss this provision in later chapters.

6. Indeed, for the interest-earning investment to pay out as much as the capital gains-earning investment, we'd need to reduce its tax rate from 20% down to 10.55%. This implies that the effective capital gains tax rate is much lower than the apparent tax rate—in the case of table 2.2, only a little more than half of the 20% tax rate that seemingly is being levied. In reality, the actual difference between the tax treatments of interest income and capital gains income is even greater, since the capital gains tax rate is much lower than the tax rate on most other forms of income.

7. If I believe my shares are going to rise back up in value, I'd want to sell the stock and realize the loss right away, but also buy the stock at the now lower price so I can hold onto that gain. The tax code has a "Wash-Sale rule" against this particular ploy.

8. Steuerle (2003).

9. For a more complete discussion of the problems inflation creates for a traditional income tax—written back when inflation was more of a problem than it is today—see Shoven (1978).

10. More precisely, the real interest rate equals (the nominal rate minus the inflation rate)/(1 + the inflation rate), so in our loan example, the real interest rate = $(1.10 - 1.00)/(1 + 1.00) = 0.05$. Typically though, for the roughly 2% inflation rates that we've experienced over the last 30 years, the simpler nominal-rate-minus-inflation is usually considered accurate enough.

11. See the discussion of tax expenditure #62 in U.S. Treasury Department (2017).

Chapter Three

The Logic of
Consumption-Timed Taxes

A traditional income tax attempts to tax all income, when it is earned. As we saw in the prior chapter, that leads to problems with pension income and capital gains income, which in turn opens the tax system up to various inequities and tax shelters.

Consumption-timed taxes are levied not when income is earned, but when it is consumed. This idea, of changing the timing of when income is taxed, is not a new one. The Cambridge economist Nicholas Kaldor, building on discussions among economists that went back to the 19th century, proposed adopting a consumption-timed income tax in 1955. There the idea languished until it was resurrected in 1974 by Harvard Law professor William D. Andrews. Studies by the U.S. Treasury Department and the British Meade Commission soon followed.[1] Since then, tax economists have studied the idea of a consumption-timed income tax extensively, and various forms have been advocated by economists and other commentators across the political spectrum.[2]

This change in timing has two rather significant impacts. The first—the primary reason why I personally advocate switching to a consumption-timed tax—is that it resolves most of the measurement issues that plague a traditional income tax. Under a consumption-timed tax, your pension income won't need to be taxed until you spend it, so there's no need to measure its size before it's actually paid out. Similarly with capital gains: if your stock portfolio has increased in value, but you haven't tapped any of it for spending, you have no consumption to tax. Waiting until you realize that gain by selling your stocks and bonds, although an anomaly under a traditional income tax, makes perfect sense under a consumption-timed tax.

In the last chapter, I noted all the "qualified" retirement accounts created to give those who don't have traditional pensions the same tax treatment as those who do. We saw that these accounts tend to undermine our current traditional income tax system. In contrast, they all make perfect sense under two types of consumption-timed taxes: an X-tax and a consumed-income tax.[3] If part of your earnings go into a traditional pension plan, or into an IRA, or 401(k), you right now are being taxed on those earnings only after you retire and begin to cash out those accounts. As we will see, converting our current tax system into a consumed-income tax would begin by expanding on those features of our tax code, and extending them in a variety of ways.

Because the timing-of-taxes issues disappear under a consumption-timed tax, a tax system built around the income-when-consumed principle is far less vulnerable to tax shelter abuses than a traditional income tax—provided we fully convert the tax system to a coherent consumption-timed tax. In a sense, the real problem with our current tax system is that it is sometimes a sort of traditional income tax (when we tax wage income and interest income and allow some interest deductions), and sometimes a sort of consumption-timed tax (when we tax pensions and capital gains). Because we currently adhere to neither standard, we have gaping inconsistencies that get exploited into tax shelters. As we saw in the last chapter, creating a consistent, coherent traditional income tax is not a feasible option. In contrast, creating a consistent, coherent consumption-timed tax *is* feasible—but only if we're willing to make all the changes needed to be fully consistent with this new logic.

There's another significant impact of the change in tax timing, from when it is earned to when it is consumed: it results in a zero effective tax rate on savings and investing. Again, as we saw in the last chapter, delaying when a tax is paid reduces the effective tax on that income. By delaying the tax on income until it is consumed, we effectively reduce the tax rate on the saving portion of income to no tax whatsoever.

To see this, suppose I earn $60,000 this year, and face a 20% consumed-income tax. If I spend it all this year, I'll owe $12,000 in taxes, and so can afford $48,000 worth of after-tax consumption, as in table 3.1.[4]

Table 3.1.   Consumption-Timed Tax

Year 1	No Saving	IRA Savings Acct
Initial Income	$60,000	$60,000
IRA Deposit		$20,000
Income Tax	$12,000	$ 8,000
Yr. 1 Consumption	$48,000	$32,000
Year 2		
IRA Withdrawal		$22,000
Income Tax		$ 4,400
Yr. 2 Consumption		$17,600

Suppose, however, that I save $20,000 this year, putting it into an IRA-type of account that earns 10% interest. I'll now owe the 20% consumed-income tax on only $40,000 this year. That $8,000 tax will leave me with $32,000 in after-tax consumption this year.

Next year, my $20,000 saved will have grown to $22,000. I withdraw the money from my qualified account, pay the 20% tax ($4,400) and consume the remaining $17,600.

Notice that by choosing to save, my after-tax consumption in the first year went down by $16,000, from $48,000 to $32,000. That gave me, after taxes, an additional $17,600 to spend the following year. So my effective after-tax rate of return to saving was 10%: $17,600 = $16,000 + $1,600. But that's exactly the same as the before-tax interest rate. Voila: under a consumption-timed tax, the effective tax rate on the return to saving is zero.[5]

This zero tax rate on savings has in turn one and perhaps two desirable effects. The first (and far more important in my estimation) is that unlike a traditional income tax, any consumption-timed tax treats all saving and investing options identically. As the last chapter showed, under traditional income tax investments with delayed tax liabilities are taxed more lightly than investments on which taxes are due immediately. That means investors have an incentive to seek out more favorably taxed investments, which are not necessarily the ones that are most productive or that generate the best before-tax returns.

In contrast, a consumption-timed tax treats all investments identically. The most productive investments, with the best before-tax returns, will always still have the best after-tax returns. The tax system will no longer distort investment decisions, which is the way it should be. This is a change that cannot help but improve economic growth.

The second possible effect (one I'm highly skeptical of) is that this zero effective tax rate on saving and investing will lead to an increase in saving and investing, also generating greater economic growth. As some proponents of this view point out, a lower tax rate on your saving/investing rate of return gives you a greater incentive to save and invest. Economists call this the "substitution effect," because the higher after-tax rate of return encourages you to save, which means you substitute spending in the future for spending now.

What these proponents of this view typically don't point out is that there's an offsetting effect, which economists term the "income effect." If you're earning a higher rate of return on your savings, you don't need to set as much aside today to meet some spending goal tomorrow. Suppose I want to retire 25 years from now, with $1 million saved up to live off in my retirement. If I can expect to earn a 6% after-tax return on my savings, I would need to save nearly $18,000 a year to reach my goal.

But if I can count on a 10% after-tax return on my savings, I would only need to save less than $10,000 a year to reach my retirement goal. So a less taxed rate of return allows you to "afford" to save less today. The evidence on how rates of returns impact savings rates is mixed, but is also generally consistent with the view that these two effects may roughly cancel each other out.

The evidence is also consistent with another view, that most people make their saving versus spending decisions while paying little if any attention whatsoever to the rate of return to saving. According to research done by behavioral economists, almost no one makes the types of careful, analytical saving decisions that underlie the "income-effect"–"substitution-effect" model of saving in the previous three paragraphs.[6] What amount did you save last year? Do you even know? Did you include the increased equity in your home? And what was your rate of return on your savings? Do you have even the foggiest idea?

Behavioral economists tell us that almost no one precisely analyzes their saving decisions, because we humans are absolutely lousy at doing that.[7] Many of us, just to be sure we save at all, force ourselves to do so automatically, by having part of every paycheck automatically put into a retirement account. But does anyone adjust their saving in response to some after tax rate of return? Do you know anyone who chose not to buy a new pair of shoes because that $12 could be earning a 7% after-tax rate of return? Neither do I.[8]

Either way, it is reasonably likely that the total amount saved and invested would not change substantially with a change in the tax system. But with that saving and investing no longer distorted by the tax system, how those savings are invested can only improve, leading to some reasonable boost in economic growth. And if the tax system were no longer open to gaming, no longer rife with inconsistencies to be exploited, we would have fewer resources wasted on constructing unproductive tax shelters. If the change were also to induce a higher savings rate and a further boost to investment and economic growth, all the better.[9]

FAIRNESS

Besides being simpler to achieve than a traditional income tax, a progressive consumption-timed tax may be seen as fairer and more consistent with some of our fundamental social principles. Taxing income when it is earned means we are penalizing productive effort, be it working, saving, investing, or running a business.

In contrast, taxing income when it is consumed levies taxes according to one's lifestyle.[10] A Warren Buffet who lives simply would be taxed simply; a

Kardashian who lives lavishly would be taxed lavishly. As a society we face two opposing impulses: the impulse to tax more those who are most well off, and the impulse to tax less those who spur economic growth.[11]

A progressive consumed-income tax retains the progressive impulse to tax those well off the most. But it calculates your tax burden not by what you contribute to the economic pie, but by the consumption you draw off from society. The entrepreneur who reinvests her earnings would be taxed relatively less; the socialite who spends profligately would be taxed relatively more.

There are many who argue that a tax system that taxes according to how much is consumed rather than how much is earned unfairly favors the wealthy, who can afford to save a larger share of their income.[12] That is a legitimate concern about any consumption-timed tax that levies the same flat rate on everyone. But a consumed-income tax is structured in many respects like a traditional income tax, with annual tax returns and a series of progressively rising tax brackets.[13]

By appropriately adjusting those tax brackets, a consumed-income tax can be exactly as progressive as a traditional income tax. Those in the top whatever percent of the income distribution would pay as a whole essentially the same share of income taxes as they pay now. Certainly, it would tax some frugal wealthy people like Warren Buffet less than under our current tax system, but it would also tax other less frugal wealthy people more than now. On average however, our current level of progressivity could be exactly maintained. And if in the process, we provide the wealthy with a greater incentive to reinvest their wealth in ways that expand our economic productivity, well, I'm OK with that.

THE CONSUMPTION TAX ALTERNATIVES

My recommendation is that we abandon the ideal of taxing-all-income-when-earned, which we saw in the last chapter has insurmountable measurement problems, and replace it with the ideal of taxing-all-income-when-consumed. Consumption-timed taxation is a framework under which cohesion is feasible. It is the framework I believe we should turn to.

There are however a number of alternative consumption-timed tax systems that we could adopt: a value added tax (VAT), a flat tax, an X-tax, or a consumed-income tax. My recommendation will be the consumed-income tax, because it is the alternative that involves the least amount of disruption; it is the alternative that is the closest to the tax system we already have (but without most of the current system's flaws). In the next chapter I will discuss the other three options.

NOTES

1. Kaldor (1955), Andrews (1974), Institute for Fiscal Studies (1978), Bradford and the U.S. Treasury Tax Policy Staff (1984).

2. See, e.g., Seidman (1997), Weisbach (2006), McCaffery (2008), Yglesias (2010), Frank (2011), Hanson (2012a), and Viard (2014).

3. The X-tax will be discussed in chapter 4.

4. There's a minor issue in how we calculate the income tax rate. $60,000 is earned, $12,000 goes to taxes, and $48,000 is spent. With an income tax, we call that a 20% tax: $12,000 taxes divided by $60,000 income. Economists call this a "tax inclusive" measure, because the $60,000 denominator includes the $12,000 that goes to taxes. Under a sales tax however, we would call the same tax a 25% tax—$12,000 taxes divided by $48,000 spent. Here our measure is "tax exclusive," since we exclude the taxes from the $48,000 denominator. The usual convention is to use the tax inclusive measure for income taxes, a convention I will stick to throughout the book.

5. With a progressive tax, the effective tax rate on savings will not always be exactly zero, but will generally be close to zero. For example, if I put $100 into my IRA when I'm 30, and in the 15% tax bracket, that saving only costs me $85 at the time. Suppose my $100 grows by 6% a year for the next 30 years, to $575.35, and I then withdraw it. But I'm now in the 25% tax bracket, so I only have $430.76 to spend after taxes. My after-tax rate of return to savings is now only 5.56%, so the effective tax rate on my return to saving is about 7%—still a rather low tax rate. Of course if my tax bracket had gone down over time instead of up, my after-tax return to savings would be above 6%, and the effective tax rate on my return to saving would be negative.

6. Frederick et al. (2002).

7. Thaler and Sunstein (2008), ch. 6.

8. Thaler (1999) suggests you may behave more frugally on bigger-ticket items.

9. A consumed-income tax also automatically resolves the issues of measuring depreciation and adjusting for inflation that bedevil a traditional income tax (Bradford et al. 1984).

10. An alternative way of stating this argument, which dates to Thomas Hobbes's *Leviathan*, is that we should be taxed not on what we contribute to society, through labor, saving, and investment, but on what we withdraw from society, through consumption. This argument was echoed by Kaldor (1955). I will discuss another more modern fairness argument, based on lifetime earnings, in chapter 9.

11. It should be noted that any form of taxation will effectively penalize working; the real distinction is whether we should penalize the saving and investment contributions to productivity.

12. This criticism of consumption taxation often focuses on the relatively light tax burden of a "wealthy miser." I will address this criticism in chapter 9.

13. An X-tax has a similar progressive rate structure.

Chapter Four

The VAT, Flat, and All That

Chapter 3 showed that re-timing taxes to coincide with consumption eliminates a number of the measurement problems that bedevil a traditional income tax. Our next step is to decide which type of a consumption-timed tax makes most sense. There are essentially four options: the value added tax (VAT), the flat tax, the X-tax, and the consumed-income tax.

THE VAT

The VAT, the flat tax, and the X-tax are all variations on the same theme. A VAT is essentially a sales tax, but one that is collected not from the consumers who buy the product, but from the businesses that produce and sell that product. The difference between taxing the consumers and taxing the businesses is more apparent than real. After all, it doesn't matter whether I sell you a $100 table, to which I then add on the $10 sales tax, or sell you a $110 table, on which I pay the government a $10 value added tax. In either case, you pay $110, I keep $100, and I send the remaining $10 to the government.[1]

A VAT would actually be collected not just from the retailer who sold you the table, but also from the manufacturer who built the table and the lumber mill that provided the wood for the table. Suppose that the table requires $20 of lumber and is sold to the retailer for $50. Then the lumber mill would owe $2 in value added taxes, raising the price of its lumber to $22. The table manufacturer would owe $5 in value added taxes on its $50 table, but would be credited for the $2 already collected on the lumber. So the table manufacturer would only have to pay $3 on the table, raising the price of the table to $55 (the original $50, plus the $2 extra it paid for the lumber and the $3 VAT it owes). Similarly the retailer would owe $10 in taxes on the sale of the table, but would be credited for the $5 already paid by the lumber mill and the manufacturer. In all, $10 in taxes would be collected on the $100 table, but it would be collected from all the businesses that contributed to the production and sale of the table in proportion to their contributions to its final sales price.

Why this complexity? Suppose the lumber company tries to sell its lumber without paying the VAT. The table manufacturer would still owe $5 in value-added taxes on its $50 table, but would no longer be credited for $2, since it would no longer have proof that the $2 was already paid in taxes. So that $5 would be collected, regardless of whether the lumber mill was being tax compliant. Just as all the W-2s and 1099s that you receive each year make it harder for you to under-report your income, the tax-at-every-level structure of a VAT helps to minimize tax cheating. Besides, businesses are required to file tax returns now; a VAT would just continue that requirement.

The primary difference between our current tax system and a VAT would be the tax treatment of wages and salaries. Employees would no longer be taxed on their earnings, but the employers would no longer be able to deduct the wages and salaries they paid. Suppose that table manufacturer paid a worker $20 to build the table. Under our current income tax, it would owe taxes on $10 of business income on the table: the $50 sale, minus the $20 for lumber and $20 for labor. Under a VAT however, its taxable "value added" is $30: the $50 sale, minus the $20 for lumber. In essence, the employer, not the worker, is being taxed on the $20 in wages. But like the non-difference between a sales tax and a VAT, this difference is also more apparent than real: it doesn't really matter whether I pay you $20, on which you owe $2 in income taxes, or pay you $18 and have to pay the government that $2 myself.[2]

Having businesses rather than employees pay the taxes on wages and salaries can be thought of either a very good thing, or a very bad thing. One clear benefit would be a gain in simplicity—millions of households would no longer have to file their Federal taxes annually.[3] A second benefit is that a VAT can easily be implemented as a destination-based tax. That is, it is easy to not tax any products that are exported, and to tax any products that are imported, so that only products that are consumed here (that is, whose final destination is the U.S.) get taxed. This ease in treating imports and exports is one of the reasons why the VAT is widely used by governments all across the world.[4]

But there are three clear downsides to the VAT. First, we would no longer have a progressive tax system: the well-off would no longer be taxed at higher rates than the just-getting-by. Every employee would be taxed at the same rate on his or her income, regardless of whether that employee is the custodian making $15,000 a year or the CEO making $15 million a year. This would occur because businesses—which would now pay the taxes on all wage and salary payments—would all be taxed at a single tax rate.

Second, tax rates would no longer be visible to the average Joe. You would be paying taxes on your income, but without a tax form to complete, you would no longer know how much you were being taxed. This downside—if it is a downside—is of particular concern to those who feel that government has grown too big. If taxes are no longer visible, voters might be less likely to resist tax increases, and tax rates might explode.

Third, eliminating household annual tax returns means eliminating all of those deductions and tax credits that households benefit from. Now, I fully agree with the perspective that we have way too many deductions and tax credits in our tax system, but that doesn't mean that we want to get rid of every single one of them. In particular, we probably want to keep the earned income tax credit, that both helps out low-income households while increasing their work incentive. We also probably want to keep the credit for child and dependent care expenses, which also increases the work incentive especially for low-income single parents, as well as the tax credits for higher education. Switching to a VAT would make keeping these, if not impossible, then at least much harder to achieve.

I would note that, other than eliminating their deduction for wages and salaries paid, the VAT treats small businesses in exactly the same way as a flat tax, an X-tax, or a consumed-income tax. We'll explore the tax treatment of small businesses in chapter 8, including the changes needed for any of these consumption-timed tax systems.

THE FLAT TAX

The Flat Tax might best be thought of as a way to achieve a VAT-like tax system without the VAT's shortcomings. Under a flat tax, businesses are again allowed to deduct wages and salaries; their employees are then taxed on that wage or salary income. That would mean all of those households would again have to file returns, but it would allow each household to have some amount of income exempt from taxation, based on the number of personal exemptions in the household. This would result in a slightly progressive tax system—more progressive than under a VAT, but less progressive than our current system. Compared to our current system however, a flat tax would still significantly shift the tax burden, away from those who are well off and onto middle-income taxpayers.

The Flat Tax, as envisioned by Hall and Rabushka, its original proposers, would have none of the deductions and tax credits that households currently benefit from.[5] Again, that could be either a very good thing or a very bad thing, depending on your perspective. Being able to file a tax return that would fit on a postcard, as Hall and Rabushka famously boasted, is an attractive idea, but in my opinion not if it means eliminating the earned income tax credit and tax credits for higher education.

THE X-TAX

The X-tax is essentially a more progressive version of the Flat Tax. As first envisioned by David Bradford, its original proposer, and as more recently proposed by Carroll and Viard, the X-tax would have the same business tax structure as the Flat Tax, with a single flat business tax rate. But it would tax households using a highly progressive series of tax rates, and would include many (but presumably not all) of the tax credits and deductions in our current tax system.[6] Carroll and Viard, in particular, recommend retaining the earned income tax credit, and leave open the possibility of retaining tax credits for child and dependent care and for higher education in their proposed version of the X-tax.[7] Because the X-tax could be designed to be as progressive as our current system, eliminating any dramatic shift in the tax burden onto the middle class, and because it would presumably retain any tax credits or deductions that we judge worth retaining, it seems to me that the X-tax is the only reasonable alternative to a consumed-income tax.

Under both the Flat Tax and its more progressive cousin, the X-tax, households would be taxed only on their wage and salary income; all other income would be taxed at the business level. That is, households would no longer have to report any interest, dividend, or capital gains income for tax purposes. This basic structure creates a number of issues.

The first involves measuring a household's standard of living. The earned income tax credit is only intended for low-income households. Under our current tax system, economic wherewithal is measured by the household's adjusted gross income (AGI), which includes not just wage, salary, or pension income and net withdrawals from qualified savings accounts, but also any interest, dividend, or capital gains income. If households no longer have to report those last three forms of income, we will no longer be able to tell who needs the assistance of the earned income tax credit and who doesn't.[8]

This issue would not just affect the earned income tax credit. Students applying for college financial aid typically have to fill out the Free Application for Federal Student Aid (FAFSA). The current form uses the parents' AGI, as reported on their most recent form 1040. Again, if we no longer have reliable information on those other forms of income, determining need will become that much harder to do.[9]

The second issue that the structure of a flat tax or X-tax creates involves the taxation of small businesses. Typically the owner of a small business earns both salary income for the time he or she spends managing the business, as well as any profits earned by the business. Under either a traditional income tax or a consumed-income tax, what portion of his or her earning we call salary and which portion profits is immaterial. Income is income, regardless of its form, and it should all be taxed the same, whether when it is earned (traditional income tax) or when it is consumed (consumed-income tax).[10]

Under an X-tax however, what we call it does matter. All wage and salary income would be taxed at a series of progressive tax rates, but all profits and other business income would be taxed at a single tax rate, typically the same rate as the highest household tax rate. That gives small business people the incentive to play the tax game of pretend-it's-all-salary-income, so their income gets taxed at a lower tax rate, as long as they're not already in the highest tax bracket.

In reality, this game really doesn't matter all that much. By playing the game, and claiming all of their income is salary income, they'd only be replicating within an X-tax what would have occurred under a consumed-income tax. All of their income, regardless of whether it really was salary or really was profits, would be taxed at the same rate. But to get to that logical result, they'd have to be playing a game, telling a fib, lying just a little on their tax returns. So essentially the X-tax has a little provision embedded in it that encourages dishonesty—not my idea of a best practice.[11]

The third and in my mind the biggest issue with either a flat tax or an X-tax is with its taxation of dividends and capital gains. Specifically, they would no longer be taxed at the household level. That would substantially reduce the tax burden on those who hold what I will be terming "old wealth"—that is, assets from saving and investing that occurred 5, 10, 20 or even 100 years ago.

Under our current income tax, corporate dividends are taxed twice, once at the corporate level, when the corporation's income is taxed, and a second time, at the individual level, when that corporate income is paid out to the individual shareholders as dividends. Under a traditional income tax, this may magnify the negative effects of taxes on the investment incentives.[12] Under a consumption-timed tax however, this double taxation has no disincentive effects whatsoever. Indeed, I will argue in chapter 11 that the double taxation of corporate dividends is an altogether desirable feature of a consumed-income tax.

But even if this double taxation were to continue to affect the incentive to create *new investment*, it would never have any effect whatsoever on the incentive to create *old wealth*, precisely because that old wealth was created years ago. Cutting—or in the case of either a flat tax or an X-tax, eliminating altogether—the personal tax rate on the returns to investments made years ago does not spur economic growth. It merely hands a tax windfall to the people who hold that old wealth, the disproportionately wealthy.[13]

Even under a consumed-income tax, it is not entirely possible to remove all of taxation's disincentive effects on new investment without creating some tax windfall for the owners of old wealth. As I will show in chapter 7, it is possible to find a reasonable balance between the two objectives. That balance would give very favorable tax treatment to almost all new saving and investment and sharply limit the windfall gain to old wealth. In contrast, under a flat tax or an X-tax, there's no attempt whatsoever to limit these windfall gains, because the basic design—tax only wage and salary income at the household level, with all other income taxed at the business level—guarantees that the full windfall must occur.

Because a VAT or a flat tax would necessarily result is a much less progressive tax system than the one we currently have, I cannot recommend them as reasonable alternatives to our current tax system. And because a VAT, a flat tax, or even an X-tax would provide the holders of old wealth with a windfall tax gain, I cannot recommend the X-tax either. That windfall tax reduction to the owners of old wealth would need to be made up somehow, presumably by taxing labor income at a somewhat higher rate, with some resulting loss in economic efficiency.

THE CONSUMED-INCOME TAX

The consumed-income tax is in my mind the best option available. A consumed-income tax is structured very much like our current income tax, with individuals paying taxes on all of their consumed income, regardless of its source. Therefore, a consumed-income tax can be as progressive (or even more progressive) than our current income tax. And as we will see in chapter 7, it is possible to transition to a consumed-income tax without creating windfall tax gains for the wealthy.

The rest of this book will examine the question of how to get there from here. Fortunately, as I suggested in the introduction, most of our current system is already consistent with a consumed-income tax, so tax reform would only involve making the remaining changes needed to get us to a coherent tax system.

The previous chapter showed that the primary differences between a traditional income tax and a consumed-income tax involve their differing treatments of saving, borrowing, and investing. In the next chapter we will begin exploring how we could convert our tax system into a consumed-income tax, by examining the consumed-income tax treatment of savings and borrowing.

NOTES

1. The example uses a 10% sales tax/VAT. If a VAT were used to entirely replace the income tax, the tax rate would probably need to be around 20%.

2. It might however make a difference for a while. If we suddenly replaced the income tax with a VAT, the tax burden on wages and salaries would be suddenly shifted to employers. The employers would probably not be able to immediately and fully cut the wages and salaries they paid to compensate for the tax shift, so for a while, the tax burden would be at least partially shifted. Over time however, we would expect smaller wage and salary increases, until the tax burden on wage and salary income has shifted back onto the employees.

3. That is the point Graetz makes in his *100 Million Unnecessary Returns* (2008).

4. Donald Trump has argued that this tax treatment, of applying the VAT to products imported from the U.S. but forgiving the VAT on products exported to the U.S., is an unfair trade practice used by many other countries to increase our trade deficit (*New York Times* 2016). Notice however that we do the exact same thing with our sales taxes. We levy a sales tax on most foreign-made products imported into the U.S., and don't levy a sales tax on any U.S.-made products sent abroad. Both our treatment of the sales tax and the foreign application of the VAT are consistent with destination-based taxation; in other words, that countries should be allowed to tax products destined for domestic consumption.

5. Hall and Rabushka (1995).

6. Bradford (2000); Carroll and Viard (2012).

7. Carroll and Viard (2012: 42 and 54–5).

8. Carroll and Viard (2012: 64) identify this as a problem.

9. Admittedly, we could ask families to voluntarily disclose those other sources of income—and if you don't suspect there would be widespread cheating, I have a nice bridge you might want to buy. Our current system makes dishonesty risky, by requiring financial firms to report to the government the same interest, dividend, and capital gains information they send to taxpayers on the various forms 1099. If we were to switch to an X-tax, it seems unlikely that this reporting would continue.

10. However, the existing payroll taxes that finance Social Security and Medicare are not levied on interest, dividend, or capital gains income, so in some cases what we call any particular part of income does currently matter. But for small businesses it currently doesn't matter: all of their small business income is subject to the payroll tax.

11. Presumably under an X-tax, small business income that is not called salary would no longer be subject to the payroll tax. That would create the opposite incentive—to understate the amount called salary income—for those small businessmen

who are within 15% of the top tax bracket. Once again there would be a strong incentive to be dishonest, but in the opposite direction.

12. However, there is a viewpoint which I ascribe to that 30 years ago was called the "New View" of dividend taxation. It argues that the second tax has no effect on the investment decisions of mature corporations. See Zodrow (1991).

13. Wolff (2017) calculated that in 2016, the wealthiest 1% of the U.S. population held about 40% of U.S. wealth, while the top 20% held nearly 90% of U.S. wealth. This wealthiest segment of the population held a disproportionate share of corporate stock. Wolff calculated that the wealthiest 1% held 31% of their wealth in corporate stock and similar financial securities, outside of IRAs and other retirement accounts, with the next 19% holding nearly 19% of their wealth in these assets. In contrast, the middle 60% of the population held only about 4% of their wealth in corporate assets, with most (87%) of their wealth held as equity in their homes, cash balances, and retirement savings accounts.

Chapter Five

Savings and Borrowing under a Consumed-Income Tax

Once we've selected the consumed-income tax as our tax reform target, many of our tax reform choices narrow considerably. Recall from the introduction that we want a tax system that is both coherent and consistent. So we want to adopt tax reforms that are consistent with the logic of a consumed-income tax, and eliminate provisions in our tax code that don't fit that logic.

That doesn't mean we have no choices left to make. But once we have an agreed-upon target, many of the choices—especially the ones in this chapter—are easy. Yes, there are still difficult decisions left, but those will come up in the later chapters.

TAX-SHELTERING ALL NEW SAVINGS

As I noted in chapter 1, a consumed-income tax taxes all income, but not until it is consumed. Our current tax system already treats a lot of income this way; that is, earnings that are saved are often exempt from taxation until they are spent. In traditional pensions, for example, the share of the worker's earnings that go into the pension plan are not taxed until the pension is paid out. Other examples include traditional IRAs and employer sponsored 401(k) savings plans, where again the earnings deposited into these accounts goes untaxed, until the savings are withdrawn from the account.

One big difference between our current tax law and a consumed-income tax is that our current law only gives this favorable tax treatment to some forms of saving. The consumed-income tax would extend this tax treatment to all forms of new saving. So currently, if you deposit money into an IRA, you can only withdraw those savings without a penalty if you are old enough to be retired, are disabled, or if you use the withdrawal to pay for major medical expenses, qualified educational expenses, or for the down payment on your first owner-occupied home.

Under a consumed-income tax, there would no longer be a need to penalize any withdrawals, because the accounts would be for all savings, no matter what the savings goal. IRAs could be tapped, without limitations, for a new home down payment, for college, for medical expenses, for a vacation, or whatever.[1] Although several of these withdrawal reasons are currently allowed, they are also currently subject to limitations. This may create problems for some families. Moving to a consumed-income tax would simplify matters entirely, by removing almost all limitations on withdrawals from these accounts.[2] The withdrawals would be taxable, but there would be no additional penalty.

Under a consumed-income tax, we would also want to substantially increase the amounts that can be contributed annually to these "tax-deferred" savings accounts. There would only be one reason to have any limit at all on how much people could deposit in an IRA-type account—to prevent the wealthy from avoiding taxes indefinitely.[3] If there were no limit, a billionaire could annually deposit just enough of her wealth into an IRA to cut her taxes to zero.[4] A reasonable limit would be a rather high annual deposit level, say $50,000 a year, that few families would ever reach.[5] Only a few families—perhaps professional athletes, who have a short but very high-paying career, and very highly paid corporate CEOs—would bump up against the limit. There would also need to be a number of exceptions to the limit that would allow you to deposit more under certain circumstances—to be discussed later.

Because tax-deferred saving accounts would be permitted for all forms of savings, there would no longer be a need to require that people withdraw from their savings accounts beginning at age 70. Savers would no longer have to choose between saving for one objective (like retirement) in one account, versus saving for another objective (like a child's college education) in another account. This is because a single account could be used for either. And no one would end up with money stranded in the wrong type of account. For instance, if Junior couldn't get into college after all, the money saved for college could be used elsewhere. One account would be enough for all and any form of saving, and the savings in that account could be used to pay for all and any legal expenditure.

LIMITING ROTH IRAS TO LOW RISK INVESTMENTS

In concept, Roth IRAs are not consistent with a progressive consumed-income tax. Under a Roth IRA, contributions are not deductible, so the taxpayer would be paying taxes on income that isn't consumed. And withdrawals are not taxed, so that future consumption would go untaxed. However, you can think of the Roth as a way to "prepay" the tax on future consumption. That is, suppose I earn $60,000 today, just as in the example in chapter 3, table 3.1.

Again, if I save nothing, the entire $60,000 is taxed today, leaving me with $48,000 to spend. Suppose, however, that I only spend $32,000 (just as in table 3.1) and save the remaining $16,000 (as in table 5.1).

Compared to the Traditional IRA treatment in table 3.1, the Roth IRA taxes me $4,000 more in the first year, and reduces my savings by that amount. That can be thought of as "prepaying" the taxes that will be owed on the saving when it gets spent next year. After earning a 10% return, my savings grows to $17,600 in the second year; since the tax has already been prepaid, I can withdraw and spend that entire amount. Notice that my second year consumption in tables 3.1 and 5.1 are exactly the same. So the Roth IRA imposes a tax level equivalent to a same-rate consumed-income tax—that is, a zero tax rate on saving.

I recommend that we retain the Roth IRA as part of a progressive consumed-income tax, but with one important modification: a limit on the types of assets held in a Roth IRA.[6] In a traditional IRA, if you invest your funds in something very risky, say gold futures contracts, and you win and get a big payoff, you can then spend (consume) a lot, and pay a lot of taxes. If, however, your portfolio goes bust, you spend nothing, and pay no taxes.[7]

Since your tax liability depends on your consumption level, it will vary with how your investments performed. But with a Roth IRA, since the taxes are "prepaid," you're taxed the same whether your investment pays off or not. Therefore, to be consistent with the spirit of a progressive consumed-income tax, Roth IRAs should only be allowed to hold low risk assets—checking and savings accounts, CDs, and money market funds.[8]

Table 5.1. Roth IRAs

Year 1	No Saving	IRA Savings Acct.
Initial Income	$60,000	$60,000
Cons. Income Tax	$12,000	$12,000
Roth IRA Deposit	$0	$16,000
Yr. 1 Consumption	$48,000	$32,000
Year 2		
Roth IRA Withdrawal		$17,600
Cons. Income Tax		$0
Yr. 2 Consumption		$17,600

In the interest of simplicity, all savings and checking accounts, CDs, and money market deposit accounts that are FDIC insured should automatically receive Roth IRA treatment. These already have limits on the type of returns they pay. Because they are FDIC insured, they are very low risk. Automatically classifying them as Roth IRAs in the first year after the tax change would merely mean that the interest earned on those accounts would become tax-free. In practice, that would be one rather small item we would no longer have to remember to report on our tax forms each year.

Because Roth IRAs do not allow any initial tax deduction, they don't create the same initial tax shelter problems as traditional IRAs. That is, even if a wealthy socialite put all her wealth into a Roth IRA, she would not be able to use that deposit to cancel out any taxes on her income this year. But it would allow her to earn tax-free interest income on all that wealth for the rest of her life. To prevent this, we would again need a cap on deposits. But it need not be an annual cap. Simpler and more appropriate would be a fixed cap on total Roth IRA assets of perhaps $250,000, which equals the limit on FDIC-insured deposits. Then any family could regularly add to or subtract from their savings, checking, CDs, and other such Roth IRA accounts. As long as the total remained below $250,000, there would be no tax consequences whatsoever.

There's an additional reason for limiting the use of Roth IRAs to common, low risk investments. A traditional IRA will generate more tax revenue than a Roth IRA on the same savings behavior without affecting savings and investment decisions at all. The traditional IRA does this by taxing "infra-marginal returns"—also called above-normal returns or excess profits.[9] I will explain this concept and give an example below.

TAXING INFRA-MARGINAL RETURNS

Imagine that most investment opportunities, like stocks or bonds, pay a 10% rate of return. Also, suppose you face a 25% consumed-income tax rate. You've earned $80,000 of wage income this year, paid $20,000 in taxes, spent $45,000, and saved the remaining $15,000 in a Roth IRA. Investing your money and earning the 10% return would give you $16,500 after one year, and $18,150 after two years.

But suppose that you have a great idea for a new software program that involves hurling one kind of animal at the glass homes of some other animal. Let's call it "Insane Armadillos." It'll take an investment of $10,000 to develop this program. If you make that investment, you'll be able to sell the program to 1 million buyers for $1 each—and net yourself a 10,000% return on your investment in one year.

Table 5.2. Roth IRA—Normal (10%) Return

Year 1	Year 1		Year 2		Year 3
Initial Income	$80,000				
25% Cons. Income Tax	$20,000				
Roth IRA Deposit	$15,000	==>	$16,500	==>	$18,150
Yr. 1 Consumption	$45,000				$18,150

But there's more. Once Insane Armadillos becomes popular, you can market all kinds of Insane Armadillo merchandising spinoffs: Insane Armadillo stuffed animals, Insane Armadillo Sweetened Corn Puffs, the Insane Armadillos Movie. The first $800,000 you invest in these ventures will earn you a 20% return the following year. But after that, you'll have saturated the market, and will get no more than the 10% return you can earn elsewhere.

If we only had Roth IRA tax treatment of savings—no deduction for saving, no tax on the proceeds—the $10,000 you invest in the software would become $1 million after one year. When reinvested, 80% in merchandise spinoffs and 20% in normal investments, it would grow to $1.18 million in the second year. Your other $5,000 in savings would just earn the 10% rate of return, growing to $6,050 in two years. So at the end of the two year period, your $15,000 in savings would have grown to $1,186,050, on average a 789% rate of return, which you could then spend tax-free (see table 5.3).

But what if your savings were put into a traditional IRA? This would allow you to save $20,000 this year, without changing your lifestyle at all. You earn $80,000 of wage income, save $20,000, pay $15,000 in taxes (25% of $60,000), and spend the remaining $45,000. In effect, when you put $15,000 of your own money into your traditional IRA, the government matched it with its own $5,000, the amount that your taxes this year went down (see table 5.4).

So now, you again invest $10,000 in Insane Armadillos, with the remaining $10,000 in normal investments that yield a 10% return. After one year, your IRA is worth $1 million from the Armadillos, and $11,000 from the

Table 5.3. Roth IRA—Insane Armadillos

Year 1	Year 1		Year 2		Year 3
Initial Income	$80,000				
25% Cons. Income Tax	$20,000				
Roth IRA Deposits	$5,000	==>	$5,500	==>	$6,050
	$10,000	==>	$800,000	==>	$960,000
			$200,000	==>	$220,000
Yr. 1 Consumption	$45,000				$1,186,050

Table 5.4. Traditional IRA—Insane Armadillos

Year 1	Year 1	Year 2	Year 3
Initial Income	$80,000		
25% Cons. Income Tax	$15,000		
Roth IRA Deposits	$10,000 ==>	$11,000 ==>	$12,100
	$10,000 ==>	$800,000 ==>	$960,000
		$200,000 ==>	$220,000
25% Cons. Income Tax			$298,025
Yr. 1 Consumption	$45,000		$894,075

other investments. You again put the $800,000 into the merchandise spinoff investments, and the other $211,000 into the stock market. So after the second year you have $960,000 from the spinoffs plus $232,100 from the stock market, a total of $1,192,100—a combined 672% rate of return.

Then you withdraw it all, and pay the 25% tax, of $298,025. That leaves you $894,075 to spend after taxes—well less than the $1,186,050 you had with a Roth IRA.

So what gives? Didn't I tell you in chapter 3 that a consumed-income tax doesn't tax the rate of return on savings? Well, it doesn't, and it does. It doesn't tax the "normal" return to savings, only the above-normal, "inframarginal" return on savings and investment.[10]

I began the story by suggesting that in this hypothetical world, most investment opportunities pay a 10% rate of return. Implied was the assumption that the supply of these investment opportunities far exceeds the amount you have available to invest. Suppose all your investment opportunities are essentially the same, all paying a 10% return. Then you will earn that same 10% return under either a Roth-IRA consumed-income tax, a traditional-IRA consumed-income tax, or no tax at all. When there's a relatively unlimited supply of identical investment opportunities, the effective tax rate on the return to saving is zero under a consumed-income tax.

To see this, let's redo the above example. Assume all the investments (including the Insane Armadillos) earn the same 10% return (table 5.5). Then with the Roth IRA, your $15,000 in savings would grow to $18,150 after 2 years, just as in table 5.2. And with the traditional IRA, your larger $20,000 in savings would grow to $24,200 before tax, and $18,150 after tax, after two years. Both are identical to no tax on your investment returns whatsoever.

The story above however gave you two special opportunities, first the software and then the spinoffs. Both limited the amount you could invest; both paid a higher rate of return. This reflects the reality that high-paying investment opportunities are few and far between and cannot be scaled up dramatically.

Table 5.5.   **Traditional IRA—Normal (10%) Return**

Year 1	Year 1	Year 2	Year 3
Initial Income	$80,000		
25% Cons. Income Tax	$15,000		
Roth IRA Deposits	$10,000 ==>	$11,000 ==>	$12,100
	$10,000 ==>	$11,000 ==>	$12,100
25% Cons. Income Tax			$6,050
Yr. 1 Consumption	$45,000		$18,150

Say you had invested in Apple or Microsoft or Facebook in their early days. You'd have made a mint. But at any particular point in time, they each had only a finite number of ways to use your investment dollars. Having all of their investors invest ten times as many dollars would have generated something less than ten times as much in earnings—a concept economists call diminishing returns.

So when, with the traditional IRA, the government matched your $15,000 with its own $5,000, and you invested those extra dollars, you faced those diminishing returns. You were only able to garner a normal 10% return on the added dollars. You still turned the first $10,000 into $1.18 million in two years. Your other $5,000 still grew to $6,050 in two years. But the $5,000 the government kicked in also grew to $6,050, for a grand total of $1,192,100, exactly $6,050 more than when you didn't get the government match.

But the government's match means that since it put one fourth of the dollars in, it gets one fourth of the dollars out. In a traditional IRA, the government becomes a silent partner, letting you make the investment decisions but demanding its share of the investment proceeds. When a portion of those proceeds are a super high rate of return, the government gets a share of those super high returns—even though its contribution only added a normal 10% return.

This is what economists call "infra-marginal" returns—infra meaning inside, so "inside the margin"—and non-economists call "excess profits." Your best investment option, the software, gave you a 10,000% rate of return. Your next best option, the spinoffs, earned a 20% rate of return. These are the returns earned "inside" the margin. All the rest of your investments, the ones "at the margin," only earn the normal 10% rate of return.

For most investors, the government's contribution will only earn the normal, marginal return. But when it takes its share, the government will be getting a portion of any above-normal, infra-marginal returns. So in effect, a consumed-income tax taxes only those investors' infra-marginal returns.

Here's the beauty of it: this generates revenue for the government without affecting your incentives whatsoever. Would you ever decide not to invest in the super-payoff software merely because the government is going to take a share of your crazy-high returns? Of course not. Maybe you would decide not to invest in the 10% return projects, if the government took a share of those. But it doesn't. So investors always take advantage of all the attractive investment opportunities they face, and the government only taxes a share of any really high returns they get lucky enough to stumble into.

This is why a consumed-income tax based on traditional-IRAs will always be superior to any tax that just exempts savings income.[11] Both will leave normal returns on savings and investment untaxed. This guarantees that the tax code will be neutral between the various investment alternatives. But the consumed-income tax will tax infra-marginal returns, generating additional tax revenue without any additional efficiency cost.[12] So a consumed-income tax can generate the same tax revenue as any savings-exempt tax, but with lower tax rates and lower efficiency costs.[13] Therefore, although Roth IRAs should be retained, they should be limited to holding generic, low-risk-low-return assets that are extremely unlikely to ever yield high, infra-marginal returns.

One additional insight: because a consumed-income tax taxes infra-marginal returns without taxing the normal return to savings, it might be free of the kind of political tug-of-war that has bedeviled our current tax system. A more progressive tax system, as favored by Democrats, would generally require a higher tax rate on the infra-marginal, above-normal return to investment. But this would have no effect on investment incentives. A tax system that does not reduce the incentives to save and invest, as favored by Republicans, would not need to be less progressive. It would be foolish to promise political harmony, but having the faint possibility of a politically stable tax system is far better than our current zero possibility whatsoever.

TAXING CONSUMER DURABLES

Consumer durables are consumption goods that last for many years, like homes and cars, boats and TVs. Technically, they are capital assets: your initial "investment" is what you pay to buy them, and their "return" is the stream of consumption services—shelter, transportation, recreation, entertainment—they provide. So under a consumed-income tax consumer durables could be treated just like IRA-type assets. That is, you could deduct what you pay to purchase the asset (the "deposit" into the asset), and then be taxed on the values of all those consumption services (your "withdrawals").

But that would be terribly cumbersome. Measuring those withdrawals—in the case of a home, the "imputed rent" mentioned earlier—would be hopelessly complex. So it's more appropriate to treat these as Roth-type assets:

no deduction for their purchase, and no tax on their consumption services. Of course, this is exactly how they are currently treated: you don't currently deduct the price of a refrigerator, and you currently aren't taxed on its use over its lifetime. So there is no need to change our tax treatment of consumer durables in switching to a consumed-income tax.

TAXING BORROWING

Under a consumed-income tax, any income that you don't spend (saving) goes untaxed until it is spent. So conversely any spending that you didn't earn ("unsaving") should be taxed when you spend it. When unsaving is a withdrawal from an IRA, it's already covered in the tax code. If, however, that extra spending is financed through borrowing, we need to take that into account.

The treatment of new borrowing that is most consistent with the logic of a consumed-income tax would be as a reverse IRA. With an IRA, the savings that goes in is deductible, and the unsaving that comes out is taxed. A consumer loan would work the same, in reverse order: the unsaving (the amount of the loan you take out) would be taxed, while the repayments (paid back in) on the loan—both principal and interest—would be deducted. Henceforth I'll refer to any debt treated this way as "taxable debt."

That fits the logic of taxing income when it is consumed, because with a consumer loan, you typically consume your income *before* it is earned. Suppose you borrow $10,000 for a trip to Tahiti this year, paying off the loan plus interest in the future. Then you have an extra $10,000 of consumption this year, but maybe $12,000 less consumption later on, when you pay off the loan. If we treat that loan as taxable debt, you would be taxed on that extra consumption this year when you took out the $10,000 loan. But you would be allowed to deduct the $12,000 in repayments from your future income, when those repayments reduce your consumption.

This tax treatment of debt is rather cumbersome, however. It would require taxpayers to include on their tax returns both the amounts borrowed (to be taxed one year) and repaid, including interest (to be deducted the next year or years). Fortunately, there's a simpler alternative.

This alternative treatment of borrowing would be as a reverse Roth IRA. With a Roth IRA, the saving that goes in is not deductible, but the unsaving that comes out is not taxed. A "Roth" consumer loan would work the same, again in reverse order: the unsaving (the amount of the loan you take out) would not be taxed and the repayments would not be deducted. This is how non-mortgage loans are currently treated. Henceforth I'll refer to any debt treated this way as "nontaxable debt."

Note that with nontaxable consumer debt, if a family bought a $20,000 car, paying $2,000 down and financing the rest with a 5 year, $18,000 loan, then (a) there would be no deduction for the $2,000. So if they withdrew that money from a traditional IRA, they'd be taxed on that $2,000.[14] Since the loan is nontaxable, (b) the $18,000 they borrowed would not be taxed. Correspondingly (c) their principal and interest payments would not be deductible. Again, this is how our tax code currently treats auto purchases, except that most people couldn't withdraw the down payment from an IRA without a penalty.[15] This is however *not* how we currently treat owner-occupied housing. But since that is such a hot-button topic, I will leave it for its own chapter.

In the interest both of simplicity and keeping the number of changes to our tax code to a minimum, I would strongly recommend that we continue this nontaxable treatment of consumer debt.

A POTENTIAL TAX SHELTER?

It might appear that allowing this nontaxable treatment of consumer debt might open up a potential tax shelter, if the loan proceeds were deposited into a traditional IRA. Suppose someone borrows $10,000, and then deposits that money into an IRA. They haven't actually saved anything. If they got a deduction for the IRA deposit but weren't taxed on the loan proceeds, they'd have a tax shelter that might let them cut their taxes to zero.[16]

Fortunately, this turns out to be a very unattractive tax shelter. Table 5.6 reworks the numbers from table 3.1 to depict this scenario. Let's say I earn $60,000. If I save nothing, I pay 20% in taxes and spend the remaining $48,000. Suppose, however, I deposit $15,000 into an IRA that earns 10% interest. The IRA deposit would reduce my taxable income to $45,000, and my 20% tax bill to $9,000. If borrowing is given Roth-IRA tax treatment, I can then borrow $12,000 (also at 10% interest) and again spend $48,000 this year.[17]

The next year, my IRA has grown by 10% to $16,500. My debt has also grown by 10% to $13,200. I empty the IRA and pay off the loan. I owe a 20% tax on the IRA withdrawal, or $3,300 in taxes. So I net the $16,500 withdrawal, minus the $3,300 tax payment, minus the $13,200 debt payment, which turns out to be a big fat zero.

Yes, I was able to delay paying $3,000 in taxes for a year. But I had to repay that tax liability, with 10% interest, a year later. And sure, this scheme would have worked in my favor if I'd been able to borrow at 5% interest and invest at a 10% rate of return. But in the real world, that higher rate of return means taking on some degree of risk, and potentially a return of less than the interest rate I'm paying on the loan. So as a tax avoidance strategy, this one

Table 5.6. A Roth Debt and Traditional IRA Tax Shelter

Year 1	No Debt/Saving	Debt & IRA
Initial Income	$60,000	$60,000
IRA Deposit		$15,000
Loan		$12,000
Cons. Income Tax	$12,000	$9,000
Yr. 1 Consumption	$48,000	$48,000
Year 2		
IRA Withdrawal		$16,500
Cons. Income Tax		$3,300
Loan Repayment		$13,200
Yr. 2 Consumption		$0

just doesn't work. So there's no need to design the tax code to prevent people from playing a game that they're (most likely) going to lose.[18]

Therefore, moving to a consumed-income tax involves almost no changes in our tax treatment of consumer debt because almost all consumer debt is already nontaxable (and hence nondeductible). We will discuss the one exception, mortgage debt, in chapter 6.

In summary, the tax code changes I recommend for household savings and borrowing are:

1. Allow (almost) all new savings to be tax sheltered:
   - Raise the annual contribution limits on tax-deferred savings accounts to $50,000;
   - Eliminate all penalties on early (i.e., pre-retirement) withdrawals and all required rates of withdrawal;
   - Eliminate redundant savings accounts (e.g., Medical SAs, Education SAs).
2. Limit Roth IRAs to low risk investments:
   - Limit Roth IRAs to holding low risk securities like FDIC insured money market accounts;
   - Automatically classify FDIC insured savings and checking accounts as Roth IRAs;
   - Cap total Roth IRA assets at $250,000.

NOTES

1. For this reason, we would no longer need "special" tax-deferred savings accounts, like Medical Savings Accounts and Education Savings Accounts. These

should all be eliminated, with existing accounts rolled over into IRAs (for MSAs) or Roth IRAs (for ESAs). However, the tax code should continue to allow for both employer-supported accounts like 401(k)s and financial institution accounts like IRAs, to provide families with convenient options for automatic savings, while retaining the option of employer matches.

2. However, if employers use matching funds to encourage long-term savings, they may want to maintain some limits on the withdrawal of savings that they have matched. We might therefore want to keep some form of limited-withdrawal 401(k) plan in the tax code.

3. This is an example of a transition issue; the transition I propose is similar the Meade committee's (Institute for Fiscal Studies 1978) "conservative" transition proposal. Transition issue will be discussed further in chapter 7.

4. The top tier of tax rates should account for this sheltering process, to maintain the desired level of progressivity.

5. Current tax law allows an individual to deposit up to $5,500 into an IRA each year, up to $12,500 into a SIMPLE (Savings Incentive Match Plans for Employees) 401(k), up to $18,500 into a SIMPLE IRA, and up to $18,000 into a 401(k). Each of these has a somewhat higher limit for individuals near retirement age, several have higher limits for employer contributions—which allow the self-employed to deposit up to $54,000 a year into a SE401(k) or SEP-IRA.

6. Graetz (1980) and Mieszkowski (1980) both make this same argument.

7. Economic theory suggests that this may actually increase risk taking, since the government absorbs some of the investment risk through the tax code.

8. There would need to be some appropriate transition rules for existing Roth IRA savings. Those rules will be discussed in chapter 7.

9. Gentry and Hubbard (1995).

10. We'll break this normal return into its four components in chapter 8.

11. Gentry and Hubbard (1995) find that these infra-marginal returns are highly concentrated among the wealthiest 5% of all households. Hence, a traditional-IRA-based consumed-income tax that taxes infra-marginal returns will be more progressive than a Roth-IRA based consumed-income tax.

12. This is one reason why in my opinion a consumed-income tax is superior to a flat tax or X-tax. Recall that the latter don't tax individuals on their investment income, effectively treating those investments as Roth IRAs.

13. To economists, the efficiency cost of a tax reflects the degree to which that tax changes desirable behavior. Suppose that taxing your work effort induces you to work less. Or suppose that taxing your investment returns induces you to save and invest less, or even to invest differently. Then an efficiency cost has been created. In general, almost all taxes create efficiency costs. But taxes are needed to finance governments. Our goal is then to design our tax system that creates as little efficiency cost as possible. So any opportunity to levy an infra-marginal tax, that generates some revenue with no efficiency cost, should be taken advantage of.

14. This is why a Roth IRA—no deduction when you deposit the money, no tax when you withdraw it—might be the preferred savings instrument for people saving for a major capital purchase, like the down payment on their first house. Since this

saving generally has a short time horizon, the low risk limitations for a Roth IRA would be appropriate.

15. The tax treatment would be different if a business purchased this car, to be used for business purposes. Chapter 8 will discuss the tax treatment of small business investments and debt.

16. Both Graetz (1980) and McCaffery (2005) discuss this issue at length.

17. $48,000 = $60,000 income − $15,000 deposit − $9,000 taxes + $12,000 loan.

18. However, the Meade committee (Institute for Fiscal Studies 1978) recommended a cap on the amount of nontaxable consumer debt. Aaron and Galper (1985) suggested a $20,000 cap which, adjusted for inflation, would be about a $50,000 cap today.

I am not particularly concerned about this strategy because (a) most of us are pretty limited in how much financial institutions are willing to lend to us, and (b) because typically we would be charged a higher interest rate on the loan than we can earn on our savings. However, given the importance of borrowing in McCaffery's (2005) "buy, borrow, and die" tax avoidance scheme for the wealthy, perhaps a $50,000 cap on nontaxable consumer debt, that almost none of us would ever reach, would be reasonable.

Chapter Six

The Tax Treatment of Owner-Occupied Housing

Homebuyers currently get no deduction for the down payment they make to buy their home. They pay no tax on the money they borrow, but they do get a deduction on their mortgage interest. And they pay no capital gains tax, indeed no tax whatsoever, on the proceeds from selling their home.[1]

This tax treatment is not consistent with either a traditional income tax, a consumed-income tax, or any other tax system, for that matter. Under the logic of a traditional income tax, the consumption stream from living in your house—the "imputed rent" discussed in chapter 2—should count as income and be taxed. So should any capital gain that occurs, every year when it occurs. Neither tax treatment is feasible, however. So we do neither, but that means home ownership is given extremely favorable treatment in our current system.

Under the logic of a consumed-income tax, owner-occupied housing could easily be treated as any other consumer durable. There would be no deductions for dollars in, and no tax on dollars out, just like a Roth IRA.[2] The dollars in would be the initial down payment, plus (a) any principal payments on the loan, and (b) any outlays on home additions, home repairs, and so on. The dollars out would be the imputed rent, plus the sale proceeds when the home is sold.[3] Since those are all the current treatments of owner-occupied housing, our current tax code is mostly consistent with a consumed-income tax.

The inconsistency arises because of the mortgage interest deduction. If we treat owning a home as a Roth IRA, we should treat the mortgage used to buy that home as a Roth (nontaxable) consumer loan, as described in the last chapter. The principal you borrow would not be taxed, but the repayments, both principal and interest, would not be deducted. So if we eliminated the deduction for mortgage interest, our tax treatment of owner-occupied housing would align exactly with the logic of a consumed-income tax.

45

Proponents of the mortgage interest deduction argue that it is needed, to encourage home ownership. Fine. But if that's our goal—to encourage more families to become homeowners—then it would be hard to imagine a worse way to try to achieve that goal. In fact, the deduction provides very little assistance to those who are at the margin, wavering between becoming homeowners or remaining renters. What it mostly does is (a) encourage well-off families to buy excessively large houses, (b) encourage families to take out home equity loans while discouraging paying off the mortgage, and (c) provide the greatest home ownership subsidy to high-income families that need it the least.

EFFECT #1

Let's take those three effects in order. First, the mortgage interest deduction encourages families to buy excessively large houses. The larger the house, the more you need to borrow. Hence the more interest you pay, the more you get to deduct, and the bigger the tax break that you get. In effect, the mortgage interest deduction lowers the cost of an extra 100 square feet of housing, making a slightly roomier McMansion all that more affordable. And as we'll see with effect #3, the tax break for that extra 100 square feet is greater for high-income households than for middle-to-low-income households.

Now, there's nothing wrong with people choosing to live in large houses, but there is something wrong with using the tax code to make that occur. It's called economic inefficiency. It arises any time the tax code distorts the price of one good, relative to all other goods.

Suppose it costs the same amount to produce strawberries and blueberries and deliver them to your local market. If their prices accurately reflect those costs, their prices will be the same, and you'll choose to buy whichever you like better. But suppose blueberries are more costly either to produce or to ship to you. Then their price should be higher, and unless you like blueberries more than strawberries, you'll choose to buy the less expensive strawberries rather than the more expensive blueberries.

Suppose, however, that the government gives a huge tax break to blueberry growers, which they in turn pass on to their customers in the form of lower blueberry prices, lower even than the price of strawberries. Now consumers will choose to buy a lot more of the more-costly-to-produce blueberries, rather than the less-costly-to-produce strawberries. If the tax break is big enough, we might even end up with people who prefer eating the less-costly-to-produce strawberries switching to the more-costly-to-produce blueberries, just because they're cheaper.

And that would be inefficient. An efficient market system satisfies the greatest preferences at the least cost. And it achieves that efficiency through prices. If blueberries cost more to produce, but I really like blueberries, enough to pay the higher price, then the market system is happy to satisfy my preferences. But if I like blueberries only a little bit more, or if I like them less than strawberries, the market system encourages me to choose the less-costly-to-produce strawberries by offering them at a lower price.

A study of the impact of the mortgage interest deduction estimated that it has resulted in roughly a 15% increase in home size—or about an extra 300 square feet.[4] So if families really want that extra 300 square feet of living space, enough to give up what it truly costs to provide it to them, then fine, let them buy it. But if they only choose that more spacious house because the tax system has artificially made it less expensive—less than the vacations or recreational vehicles or music lessons or whatever else they would have bought had they faced the true cost of that extra housing—then no, we shouldn't be distorting their buying decisions by artificially making one consumer good—housing—cheaper than all the other goods they might buy.

EFFECT #2

The mortgage interest deduction encourages families to take out home equity loans, while discouraging paying off the mortgage. This is its second undesirable effect. It does this because the more you owe on your mortgage (up to $1 million), the bigger your tax break.[5]

Consider our recent history with housing prices. Overly easy-to-get mortgages helped produce a bubble, followed by a price collapse. Millions of families discovered that they owed more than their home was worth. Given that history, encouraging people to owe as much as they possibly can on their homes seem like a very bad idea. But that is what our current tax system continues to do.

Because the mortgage interest deduction creates an incentive to hold as large a mortgage as possible, it's absolutely incompatible with a consumed-income tax. Suppose you're paying 6% interest on your mortgage, but a low risk investment only earns you a 5% return. If you have any spare cash, the smart thing to do would be to use it to pay down your mortgage, saving yourself a 6% interest payment, rather than merely earning 5%. This same logic holds if mortgage interest is deductible—as long as the investment earnings are taxable. A 25% tax rate would reduce both the effective mortgage interest rate you pay, and the after tax investment return you earn, both by one fourth. So you'd still be better off paying down your mortgage, saving yourself a

Table 6.1.   Paying Off Mortgage vs. Low Risk Investment

	Investment Return	*Mortgage Interest Rate*
No Tax	5.00%	5.00%
25% Income Tax	3.75%	4.50%
Mortgage Deduction/IRA	5.00%	4.50%

4.5% after-tax-deduction interest payment, rather than earning only an after-tax return of 3.75% (table 6.1).

But tax-deferred savings accounts like IRAs totally change that calculation. If you can put your spare cash into an IRA, and earn a 5% rate of return, that return will not be taxed. If you use your spare cash to pay down your mortgage, and the interest is still deductible, you only save yourself from paying a 4.5% after-tax-deduction interest rate. It now becomes "smart" to borrow as much on your home as you can, putting the loan proceeds into an IRA. But this is exactly the kind of behavior we don't want our tax code to encourage.[6]

Mortgage debt is also widely used, especially by high-income households, as an indirect way to get a tax break for borrowing for other, non-housing consumption.[7] This effectively provides them with a loophole, through which they can effectively reduce the tax they pay on their consumed income.

But the whole point of my proposed tax reform is to create a coherent tax system that is not open to such manipulation. The mortgage interest deduction is not consistent with a consumed-income tax. So if we want a tax system that actually makes sense, the mortgage interest deduction must go.[8]

EFFECT #3

The mortgage interest deduction provides the greatest home ownership subsidy to high-income families that need it the least. This is its third undesirable attribute, especially if we think of it as a tool for encouraging more families to become homeowners. Let me give a simple example, using the 2017 tax code.

Consider two families, the Smiths and the Brangelinas. The Smiths together earned $60,000 in 2017, and had just bought a $250,000 home. They had a $220,000, 5% mortgage, on which they paid $11,000 in interest. When they added that to their itemized deductions, it pushed their total deductions to $19,700. But since their 2017 standard deduction was $12,700 that only reduced their taxable income by $7,000.[9] They were in the 15% tax bracket, so because of the mortgage interest deduction they saved $1,050 in taxes in 2017 (table 6.2).

Table 6.2. **Mortgage Interest Deduction Relative Benefits**

	Smiths	Brangelinas
2017 Income	$60,000	$20,000,000
Non-Mortgage Deductions	$8,700	$500,000
Standard Deduction	$12,700	$12,700
Deduct w/o Mortgage	$12,700	$500,000
Mortgage	$220,000	$750,000
Mortgage Interest	$11,000	$37,500
Deduct w/ Mortgage	$19,700	$537,500
Added Deduction from Mortgage	$7,000	$37,500
Mortgage Deduction Tax Savings	$1,050	$13,125

The Brangelinas earned $20 million in 2017. They had two homes, one in Beverly Hills and the other in Aspen, with a combined mortgage of over $1 million. They were allowed to deduct the interest on the first $750,000. They paid 5% interest, or $37,500 in deductible interest that year. Their other deductions were already more than the standard deduction, so the mortgage interest deduction reduced their taxable income by the full $37,500. They were in the 35% tax bracket, so because of the mortgage interest deduction they saved $13,125 in taxes in 2017.

The mortgage interest deduction encouraged the Smiths to become home-owners, by reducing their tax liability by $1,050 if they did. And it encouraged the Brangelinas to become homeowners, by reducing their tax liability by $13,125 if they did.

Economics research backs up this example. Studies consistently find that the overwhelming majority of benefits from the mortgage interest deduction accrue to very high-income households.[10] They also find that either eliminating the mortgage interest deduction, or replacing it with some reasonable alternative, would substantially increase the progressivity of our tax system.[11]

Does anything here seem a little wrong to you? Do the Brangelinas need over 12 times more encouragement to become homeowners than the Smiths? Are high-income people particularly averse to homeownership? Or is the mortgage interest deduction a particularly poorly designed tool, targeting almost all its encouragement at those who need it the least?

I would argue that it's the latter. And I would note that because the 2017 Tax Cuts and Jobs Act (TCJA) raised the standard deduction to $24,000, today the Smiths would get absolutely no tax break from the mortgage interest deduction whatsoever—but the Brangelinas would still get that $13,125 reward for becoming homeowners.

I do not oppose the idea of encouraging home ownership. But if we are going to use the tax code to encourage home ownership, it should not be done in a way that pays people to live in excessively large houses. It should not be done in a way that rewards people for carrying too large a mortgage. And it should not be done in a way that gives the most assistance to those who are well off, who will probably be homeowners no matter how we structure the tax system, rather than to moderate income households, who are more likely to be on the fence.

WHAT IT DOESN'T DO

But perhaps most importantly, we should encourage home ownership in a way that actually works. Because the mortgage interest deduction appears to be *totally* ineffective at increasing homeownership.

Economists consistently find that the mortgage interest deduction has no effect whatsoever on the percent of households who own their own homes.[12] This is partly because banks capture a share of the deduction's benefits, through higher mortgage interest rates.[13] This is also partly because the deduction drives up home prices, pricing especially younger households out of the market.[14]

It should not be all that surprising that the mortgage interest deduction doesn't work. Even if it weren't partly siphoned off by banks, or mostly offset by higher house prices, a subsidy that primarily targets high-income households (already likely to become owner-occupants) is not going to have much of an impact. So once again, if the goal is to encourage more families to become homeowners, then it would be hard to imagine a worse way to try to achieve that goal.

SO, WHAT TO DO?

Again, let's suppose that our goal really is to encourage more families to become homeowners. If we want to do it effectively—that is, through something other than the mortgage interest deduction—how should we go about it?

Two options are frequently put forward. One involves replacing the mortgage interest deduction with a mortgage interest tax credit, which would retarget its benefits more toward middle-income households. This first option generally seems to be effective at reducing the overall tax subsidy to owner-occupants. But it seems to have little to no impact on homeownership rates.[15]

The other option would replace the mortgage interest deduction with some type of fixed (that is, not interest-related) refundable tax credit.[16] Unlike the first option, this refundable first-time homebuyer tax credit appears to boost homeownership rates substantially.[17] It's not hard to understand why. If you think back to when you first became a homeowner, you might remember how tough it was to come up with a down payment, and how difficult the monthly mortgage payments were for the first few years. Then, as your income gradually increased and inflation reduced the real cost of those monthly payments, keeping up with the mortgage got easier and easier.

An interest tax deduction or interest tax credit that you get in your 10th year of homeownership is worth next to nothing in the year you're trying to become a first-time homebuyer. In contrast, a big, immediate tax break could make all the difference in the world. If our goal really is to encourage home ownership through our tax code, it would make sense to structure that tax break to be as effective as possible. And if our goal is to have a tax system that is consistent and coherent, we should purge it of anything that rewards more borrowing.

For both reasons, I strongly recommend that we replace the mortgage interest deduction for all new homebuyers with a first-time homebuyer tax credit.[18]

PRE-EXISTING MORTGAGES

For pre-existing mortgages, the existing deduction should be converted into a mortgage interest tax credit, at a rate somewhere between 12% and 20%. In Table 6.2, if a 20% tax credit replaced the deduction, the Smiths would get a $2,200 tax break (20% × $11,000) and the Brangelinas a $7,500 tax break (20% × $37,500)—still quite unequal, but substantially less so. This mortgage interest tax credit could then be phased out over a 20-year period.

I fully recognize that the mortgage interest deduction has been, and probably continues to be, a sacred cow that politicians are reluctant to meddle with. So making the changes I'm recommending will almost certainly be an uphill climb. But it ultimately comes down to one decision: do we want a coherent, cohesive tax system or not? If the answer is no, that we're just fine with the mess we have, then you should just stop reading right now.

But if the answer is yes, we need a tax system whose parts all fit together in a logical, coherent fashion, then we only have one choice: the mortgage interest deduction should absolutely be eliminated.

In summary, the tax code changes I recommend for owner-occupied housing are:

1. Give all consumer debt Reverse-Roth (nontaxable) treatment:
   - Eliminate the mortgage interest deduction for new mortgages;
   - Convert the mortgage interest deduction for old mortgages into a tax credit, to be phased out over 20 years;
   - Provide new, first-time homebuyers with a fixed, refundable tax credit.

NOTES

1. This capital gains exclusion only applies to the primary residence, not to a second home, and only to the first $500,000 in capital gains for a married couple. In other words, it applies to almost all of us.

2. Since the return on owning this asset is primarily the consumption stream from living in the house, it is a mostly low risk asset, so giving a home Roth IRA tax treatment would be consistent with the restriction that Roth IRAs only hold low risk assets.

3. I will discuss in further detail the tax treatment of any capital gain on the home in chapter 12.

4. Hanson (2012c).

5. Dunsky and Follain (2000) estimated the responsiveness of mortgage debt to its after-tax price. Their results suggest that eliminating the mortgage interest deduction would reduce the mortgage debt held by high-income households by about 70%, while reducing the mortgage debt held by all other households by about 20%. Overall, mortgage debt would fall about 30% (my calculations, based on their tables 4 and 5). Similarly, Gervais and Pandey (2005) estimate that eliminating the mortgage interest deduction would lead taxpayers overall to lower their loan-to-home value ratio by 25 percent.

6. Maki (1996) discusses the problems that continuing to allow a mortgage interest deduction under a consumed-income tax would create. He notes that, because of their financial sophistication, primarily high-income households would reap the benefits of using tax-deductible mortgage debt to finance tax-sheltered investments.

7. Skinner and Feenberg (1990) were one of several studies to find that after the 1986 tax reform eliminated the deductibility of non-mortgage consumer interest, for every dollar consumer interest decreased for high-income households, their mortgage interest increased by about 77 cents (see the literature review in Maki [1996]).

8. Steuerle (2003) provides an interesting tongue-in-cheek illustration of why, if we wish to broaden the tax-sheltered treatment of saving, we absolutely must eliminate the tax-favored treatment of borrowing. That necessarily includes the mortgage interest deduction.

9. Follain and Ling (1991) point out that the standard deduction reduces the value of the mortgage interest deduction for many owner-occupants, and eliminates it entirely for the typical low-to-moderate income household. For them, it is essentially a "wasted deduction."

10. Poterba and Sinai (2008) found that in 2003, the average tax savings from the mortgage interest deduction was over $6,000 a year for households earning $250,000 a year or more, but only about $200 a year for households earning $40,000 a year or less. Cole, Gee and Turner (2011) found similar results for the 2007 tax year, when the highest earning 5% of the population received roughly 37% of all the tax savings from the mortgage interest deduction.

11. Anderson and Roy (2001) estimate that eliminating the mortgage interest deduction would, with no other changes, increase one measure of progressivity, the Suits index, by about 50%. Cole, Gee and Turner (2011) find that replacing the

mortgage interest deduction with a 15% refundable tax credit on the first $25,000 of interest expenses would increase the average tax benefit for households making under $75,000.

12. Hilber and Turner (2014) found that the mortgage interest deduction has "no discernible impact" on the level of U.S. homeownership. Using an index of metropolitan-area housing regulations, they found that in metropolitan areas with relatively tight restrictions, the mortgage interest deduction itself only led to higher housing prices, with no increase in owner-occupancy. In metropolitan areas with relatively loose restrictions, they found that the mortgage interest deduction does increase owner-occupancy, but only for higher-income households.

13. Hanson (2012b) found that roughly one-eighth of the owner-occupied housing subsidy created by the mortgage interest deduction went to mortgage lenders rather than owner-occupants.

14. Bourassa and Yin (1999).

15. Binner and Day (2015).

16. The President's Advisory Panel on Federal Tax Reform (2005) proposed a tax credit equal to 15% of mortgage interest paid, capped at the interest on a mortgage limited to the average regional price of housing (limits ranging from about $227,000 to $412,000). The Simpson-Bowles National Commission on Fiscal Responsibility and Reform recommended replacing the deduction with a 12% non-refundable mortgage interest tax credit, capped at a $500,000 mortgage, available only for the primary residence (Moment of Truth 2010). Eng (2014) examines four options: a 15% non-refundable mortgage interest tax credit, a 20% non-refundable mortgage interest tax credit, a refundable property tax credit, and a fixed refundable credit of about $800 a year for all homeowners. Gale, Gruber and Stephens-Davidowitz (2007) proposed a first-time homebuyer tax credit. One was enacted as part of the American Recovery and Reinvestment Act of 2009, and expired in 2010.

17. Green and Vandell (1999) estimated that replacing the mortgage interest deduction with a fixed tax credit of $800 to $1,000 per year would boost the overall homeownership rate by 3 to nearly 5 percentage points. Homeownership among low-income households might rise even more, by 6 to 8 percentage points. Binner and Day (2015) estimated that a first-time homebuyer tax credit, modeled on the one proposed by Gale, Gruber and Stephens-Davidowitz (2007), would increase overall homeownership by about 21 percentage points. Bourassa et al. (1994) estimated that the elimination of a first-time tax credit in Australia reduced homeownership rates among young people by almost 9 percentage points.

18. Harris et al. (2013) discuss several other options for replacing the mortgage interest deduction with a non-debt related homebuyer tax subsidy.

Chapter Seven

Transition Issues

As quite a few tax economists have pointed out over the last 40 years, it's easy to describe how a consumed-income tax would work after it's completely phased in. But figuring out the phase in, the tax transition, how we get from where we are to where we want to end up, that's the challenge.[1]

Any change in the tax system creates some transition issues, where people are suddenly confronted with a change in how the tax rules treat them. To see the main transition issue with a consumed-income tax, imagine a simplified world with only two types of people. The first are young workers, who spend most of their paychecks when they earn them, but save a bit each year for their retirement. The second are old retirees, who live off those accumulated savings, plus the income those savings bring them. Under a traditional income tax, the young workers would be taxed primarily on their wage income, with maybe a bit of savings income to pay taxes on; the old retirees would only pay taxes on their savings income.

Suppose, however, that the tax system were suddenly changed to either a national sales tax, or to a value added tax (VAT). The young workers would immediately experience a small tax reduction, since they would no longer be taxed on that little bit of wage income that they are saving rather than spending. Eventually, they'll pay taxes on that wage income too, but not until they're retired, and are spending down their savings.

The old retirees would however immediately face a large tax increase. Under the traditional income tax, they'd been paying taxes on the interest and capital gains they'd received from their savings. But they didn't have to pay taxes on the original savings itself—which after all was taxed as wage income, way back when they were young. Now though, all of their spending would be taxed, including any old savings they need withdraw to finance their retirement lifestyle.

Switching to a sales or value added tax would impose a windfall loss on the older generation, by creating a tax liability that they hadn't prepared for. And that, I think we'd all agree, would be unfair.

Now imagine that instead of a sales-type tax, the tax system were suddenly changed to a wage tax that exempts savings income. The old retirees would suddenly have no tax liability whatsoever, and so a windfall tax gain. To make up for the reduced tax base, tax rates would need to be higher—so the young workers would face an immediate tax increase (which would be partly offset after they retire, when they too would owe no taxes). Again, the result would not be particularly fair. Plus, this tax windfall for the elderly would affect the work incentives of the younger generations.[2]

Simulations done by a number of economists have found that these two alternatives create enormously different "intergenerational transfers," and that the impacts of these transfers persist well into the future.[3] The sales tax transition, by imposing an extra tax burden on the elderly, would make all future generations better off by taxing them less, leaving them with more after-tax income to save and invest. This would also result in a larger future stock of productive capital. The wage tax transition, by forgiving the elderlies' tax burdens, would make the younger generations worse off, for the same reasons in reverse. So which option should we choose?

Fortunately, there is a third option. If, in this simple world I've described, we suddenly introduce IRAs that the young workers could put their savings into, continue to tax the old retirees as they had been under the income tax, and limit the old retirees' ability to put their accumulated savings into IRAs, these intergenerational transfers would be nearly zero.[4] So that is the transitional strategy that I am recommending in this chapter.[5]

Specifically, I recommend that all "old wealth"—that is, non-IRA wealth accumulated up until the tax change, under the existing tax system—continue to get the current tax treatment with a relatively small number of changes, until that wealth is passed on to the next generation.[6] That will ensure that the holders of that wealth get neither too much of a windfall gain, nor bear too much of a windfall loss.[7] However, any pre-reform special tax treatment that is inconsistent with both the logic of a traditional income tax and that of a consumed-income tax will be considered fair game.[8] I begin with the easiest transition rules: the ones that would apply to almost all of us.

CONSUMED-INCOME TAX
TRANSITION FOR MOST FAMILIES

Moving to a consumed-income tax holds the number of changes down to just those needed to rationalize our tax system, and so keeps those transition issues to a minimum. That's a major advantage of a consumed-income tax, compared to other tax reform proposals. The switch to a national sales tax, a value added tax, or a flat tax would dramatically increase the tax burdens of the households in the lower two-thirds of the income distribution. High-income households would experience windfall gains, as their income from decisions made long ago would be taxed at significantly lower rates. And, as we saw above, switching to a sales or value added tax would greatly raise the tax burden on the elderly, imposing on them a large windfall loss. They are mostly exempt from income taxes, but would find the costs of their purchases increased significantly under the new tax.

In contrast, for most families the switch to a consumed-income tax would present almost no transition issues whatsoever. Almost all of our accumulated wealth is in pension plans, IRAs, 401(k)s, and home equity, all of which would be kept, but simplified, by these reforms.[9] Most non-IRA CDs, savings, and checking accounts would automatically be given Roth IRA status. Since most families have less than $50,000 in non-IRA investment accounts, these savings could be fully transferred into new IRA accounts immediately. There would be no tax changes to any existing debt, other than mortgage and student loan debt.

The primary transition issue for most families would have to do with their mortgage. Under the logic of a consumed-income tax, the interest on new mortgages should not be deductible. I recommended in chapter 6 that for pre-existing mortgages, the interest deduction be replaced with a mortgage interest tax credit, at a rate somewhere between 12% and 20%. That would benefit the majority of existing homeowners. Only households in the top tax brackets would face a reduced tax break. As I argued earlier, the current tax code excessively rewards them for home ownership. So the change would be reducing an inequity, not creating one.

The other common transition issue for most families would involve student loans. As I will discuss in chapter 12, the deduction of student loan interest, like the deduction of mortgage interest, is incompatible with a consumed-income tax. I recommend eliminating the deduction twenty years after the switch to a consumed-income tax is adopted. That would give the most recent graduates at that time twenty years of interest deductions; graduates the next year nineteen years of deductions, and so on.

EXISTING ROTH IRAS

With the change in tax law, some families would find that their existing Roth IRAs violate either the $250,000 cap on Roth IRAs, or the limit on the types of assets allowed in Roth IRAs (see chapter 5). One way to handle this would be to have transition rules that allow a full rollover into a traditional IRA, above and beyond the $50,000 annual limit on IRA contributions, while allowing a reasonable amount of time, say five years, for this to be accomplished.

Better would be to grandfather these pre-existing Roth IRAs, but require any new deposits to meet the new tax rules. If an existing Roth IRA exceeds the $250,000 limit, no new savings could be deposited into the account. However, any earnings from the existing Roth IRA assets—like dividends on the stocks held in the Roth IRA—could continue to accumulate. But those new accumulations would need to be held as low-risk assets.[10]

Those grandfathered assets could then continue to be held as stocks, bonds, mutual fund shares, or whatever other form they were in when the new tax rules came into play. However, if any of these assets are sold, traded, or come to maturity, the funds from the sale must then meet the limit on the types of assets allowed. So if you currently hold a stock portfolio in your Roth IRA, you could continue to hold it as stock. But if you sold any of the stock, you'd need to deposit the proceeds in a savings account, CD, or money market account, or deposit up to $50,000 into a traditional IRA. In addition, some sunset clause on the grandfathered assets would be appropriate. Perhaps after ten years, all Roth IRAs would need to meet the $250,000 limit, and all Roth IRA assets would need to be low risk.[11]

TAX TRANSITION FOR OLD WEALTH

The biggest transition issues would only affect a small minority of households, those with substantial "old wealth" assets above and beyond their home and any existing IRA-type of account. As we saw above, in defining our transition rules, we need to balance the goal of not imposing too hefty a tax on old wealth with the goal of not providing too big a windfall to the owners of old wealth. I suggest we adopt the following guiding principles for developing our transition rules:

- *Allow old wealth to gradually transition into IRA status, without letting the wealthy shelter most or all of their consumption from taxation.*

The $50,000 annual limitation on IRA deposits is itself a way of addressing a transition issue. In theory, a consumed-income tax should have no limits on IRA deposits whatsoever. If we only want to tax consumed income, all saved income should be tax-free until it is consumed. But moving pre-existing savings into an IRA isn't really "saving." So a reasonable solution is to limit the amount of old wealth that can be moved into an IRA account, thereby allowing old wealth to gradually migrate into IRAs at a controlled rate.

The $50,000 cap on deposits into IRAs would allow most households to quickly move all of their non-IRA wealth into IRAs. Any household with about $60,000 or more in annual income would be able to shift close to $500,000 into IRAs in 10 years—and there are very few families that have that much wealth outside of their home and their pension fund. The only households that would not be fully transitioned within a short period of time would be the very wealthy.[12]

It is primarily the latter group that creates transition issues. We can't just let them deposit their wealth into IRAs without limitation, because much of their wealth would currently be taxed as capital gains. To see the problem, consider the case of a millionaire playboy who has an inherited stock portfolio currently worth $40 million. He earns $500,000 a year in dividends on his stock, and spends it all to maintain his lavish lifestyle. His stock portfolio was valued at $20 million when he inherited it, so if he sells any stock, half the sale proceeds are the untaxable cost basis of his stock.[13]

If there were no limit on IRA deposits, this millionaire could sell $1 million a year of his stock portfolio, and deposit the proceeds into an IRA. He could then buy the stock back within the IRA. He would then owe taxes on his $500,000 dividend income, plus the capital gain on his stock sale, minus the IRA deposit. But since that $1 million stock sale would have a $500,000 cost basis, his taxable capital gain would be only $500,000.

He would then owe taxes on the $500,000 dividend income, plus the $500,000 capital gain, minus the $1 million IRA deposit—that is, no taxes whatsoever. If there were no limit on IRA deposits, our millionaire could consume a half a million dollars a year without paying any taxes at all, for the next 40 years, merely by shifting $1 million a year into his IRA (table 7.1).

This problem arises because of the way a traditional income tax treats capital gains. When you sell the asset, only the gain is taxed. So if the entire sale proceeds could be deposited into an IRA, both the original basis and the

Table 7.1. The Millionaire's Annual Tax Return, No IRA Cap

Dividend Income		$500,000
Stock Sales Proceeds	$1,000,000	
Minus Stock Basis	−$500,000	
Capital Gains Income		$500,000
Minus IRA Deposit		−$1,000,000
Taxable Income		$0

capital gain would be deductible. But only the gain would be taxed, resulting in a negative tax liability. And it's this negative tax liability that this million-aire would be using to shelter all of his consumption for 40 years.

To be fully deductible, IRA deposits can't exceed taxable income, so if there were no cap, all of the taxable gain could be deposited, but not the untaxed basis. But that still wouldn't prevent this millionaire from avoiding taxes altogether. After all, he had nearly a $1 million in taxable income—the $500,000 dividend income, plus the $500,000 capital gain, minus a personal exemption and any deductions. Limiting him to depositing only his taxable income would still allow him to shelter all of that income in an IRA, while still consuming his $500,000 of untaxed basis.

So I recommend that we impose a $50,000 cap. For this millionaire that means he would probably never fully migrate his wealth into an IRA. But when he dies, the inheritances his heirs receive would be fully taxable, and fully IRA eligible. So eventually, because the consumed-income tax would tax inheritance income, all of this millionaire's remaining wealth would be allowed to transition into an IRA.[14]

• *Tax the income from old wealth as much as possible under current income tax rules (i.e., grandfather old wealth).*

Capital gains on non-IRA assets would still be taxed on realization. Pre-existing business assets would still be depreciated. The interest on pre-exist-ing business loans would continue to be deductible, but not the principal.[15] Eventually, all the pre-existing loans would be paid off, the pre-existing assets fully depreciated, and the assets with accrued capital gains would be passed on as inheritances. So eventually, all these rules could be eliminated. But in the meantime, by keeping the old rules in place as much as reasonably possible, and continuing to tax old wealth under those rules, we minimize the windfall gains and losses that can occur in any tax transition.

This is not to say all windfalls can be prevented. Suppose I own an old restaurant, and am depreciating my business assets. If you open a brand new restaurant, you would be allowed to expense your business assets. You would be getting a somewhat more favorable tax treatment than I get. That would in effect reduce the market value of my business somewhat.

But these kinds of changes in value are a normal part of business life, and cannot be prevented. Nor should we try to eliminate them. After all, the same thing would happen if you were able to incorporate some new technology into your new business that I don't immediately adopt, because I don't want to throw away my previous investment in all of my old-technology equipment. Change happens, and asset prices respond. We don't want to create any more of these assets adjustments than we have to, but when they occur, so be it.[16]

Nevertheless, we would want to make three changes in how we treat the income derived from old wealth. The first change would delay taxing any capital gains that are reinvested, rather than consumed. By adding a "rollover" provision to the tax code, investors could sell shares and reinvest in other securities without being taxed. That currently occurs within IRAs—when you buy and sell shares within the IRA, and as long as nothing is withdrawn, you pay no tax. This change would extend that tax treatment to investments outside of IRAs.[17]

Second, one of the tax games that sophisticated investors currently play involves "realizing losses." That is, they shelter income by selling assets that lose value, while holding onto assets that gain value. Rolling over gains without plugging this hole would create an even bigger loophole for avoiding taxes. So a new rule, allowing capital losses only to offset realized capital gains, would be needed. Capital losses could be carried forward, as under current law. However, capital losses should no longer be allowed to offset other income.[18]

The third change would be to eliminate the current tax law's lower tax rates on dividend and capital gain income.

* *The income from old wealth should be taxed at the same rates as other forms of income, even if it currently receives more favorable tax treatment.*

If a wage earner spending $70,000 a year pays a 20% tax on her consumed income, the tax rate our millionaire pays on his consumed income should be at least as high, if not higher. That will often not be the case, since any consumption the millionaire finances by selling off old wealth will be taxed only on the capital gain the old wealth has accumulated. That means that in general, our measure of the consumption enjoyed by those holding old wealth will be too low.

This error in under-measuring their consumption should not compound by taxing that under-measured consumption at too low a rate. In particular, the current very low tax rates on both dividend and capital gains income, which are not at all consistent with the logic of a traditional income tax, are even less consistent with the logic of a consumed-income tax. Therefore, both dividend and capital gains income from old wealth should be taxed at the same rates as all other forms of income.[19]

In summary, the transition tax rules I recommend are:

1. Eliminate special tax treatments:
   * Tax dividend and capital gains income earned outside of tax-deferred savings accounts at the same tax rate as other consumed income;
   * Allow capital gains to be rolled over into new investments, but only allow capital losses to offset realized capital gains.

2. Give all consumer debt reverse-Roth (nontaxable) treatment:
   • Eliminate the deduction of student loan interest payments, 20 years after enactment.
3. Transition rules:
   • Grandfather existing Roth IRAs assets, but require any new deposits, account earnings, and asset exchanges to meet the new tax rules.

NOTES

1. E.g., Mieszkowski (1978) and Bradford (1980). For a comprehensive discussion of transition issues, see Sarkar and Zodrow (1993).

2. One of the problems with an X-tax, as originally proposed by Bradford (2005) and most recently advocated by Carroll and Viard (2012), is that it would forgive much of the accumulated tax liability on old wealth. The X-tax would be made up of a single-rate tax on all businesses, and a progressive wage tax on individuals. As a result, adoption of an X-tax would wipe out all the taxes that would have been owed by wealthy individuals on their dividends and capital gains income.

3. Summers (1981), Auerbach and Kotlikoff (1983, 1987), Seidman (1984).

4. See McGee (1989). Seidman (1984) explored a transition wherein all individuals above a certain age at the time of the tax change continued to pay the old income tax, and everyone else would pay the new consumption tax—a similar idea, but not particularly practical.

5. The Meade committee's (Institute for Fiscal Studies 1978) "conservative" transition treatment would allow non-IRA old wealth to gradually migrate into IRAs, with a strict limit on the migration rate (1191–192). They also recommended that the income from this non-IRA old wealth be taxed as under an income tax (177). That is my recommended strategy in a nutshell.

6. We'll look at the issues of inheritances and bequests in chapter 9.

7. Stiglitz (1985) suggested treating old wealth as "partially registered" assets, whose original basis can be deducted when they are consumed. Minarek (1985) agreed, but stressed the administrative complexity of this approach. Aaron and Galper (1985) recommended that the original, deductible basis be adjusted to reflect a normal rate of return after the tax change.

All of these approaches add considerable complexity, and are really unnecessary. After all, the owners of old wealth acquired that wealth under the rules of an income tax. Fairness dictates only that they not have those rules yanked out from under them, not that they necessarily gain access to the new rules that new saving gets under the tax reform. After all, if you buy a car, and pay for it in full, fairness dictates that the auto company not attempt to charge you any more than you agreed to pay for it; fairness does *not* dictate that if they cut the sticker price, you should get a rebate on the price you'd previously agreed to.

8. Graetz (1980) argues against special transition rules when especially favorable tax treatment is taken away.

9. Saez and Zucman (2016) estimated that the middle class—the group between the 50th and 90th percentiles in the wealth distribution—hold about 70% of their net wealth in pension plans, IRAs, and 401(k)s, with the rest nearly evenly divided between business assets and home equity. They also noted that the bottom 50% of the wealth distribution holds almost no net wealth at all. Similarly, Wolff (2017) found that his middle wealth class—the group between the 20th and 80th percentiles—held about 87% of their wealth in home equity, retirement savings, and bank deposits.

10. The easiest way to administer this would be for the individual to have two Roths at the same financial institution, one grandfathered and the other compliant, with any earnings in the grandfathered account other than capital gains automatically deposited into the compliant account.

11. A high-income individual with up to $750,000 in a Roth IRA when the tax change occurred could move the excess $500,000 in assets to a traditional IRA over that 10 year period.

12. Since IRA deductions could not reduce tax liability below zero, the effective cap for many families would be their taxable income.

13. Normally the cost basis would be what he paid for the stock. But if he inherited the stock, his basis is the value of the stock the day his last parent died—even if his parents had purchased the stock portfolio for only $1 million, due to the capital gains "stepped up basis" provision.

14. We'll discuss the issues of inheritances and bequests in chapter 9.

15. These loans would need to be continually paid off in a timely fashion to retain interest deductibility.

16. Bradford (1986) suggested that the increase in saving and investment induced by a switch to a consumed-income tax would lower before-tax rates of return on old wealth, offsetting any forgiveness of tax liabilities on capital income. Carroll and Viard's (2012) entire discussion of the transition to a consumed-income tax focuses on the capital losses imposed on old wealth holders by these lower before-tax rates of return. However, their claims are contradicted by the simulations by Summers (1981), Auerbach and Kotlikoff (1983, 1987), Seidman (1984), and McGee (1989), who all found that forgiving the expected tax liabilities on old wealth created a huge transfer to these old wealth owners. Implicit in the simulations was the fact that the creators of all the new savings benefitting from the tax change would for the most part be themselves the owners of that old wealth.

17. The Meade committee (Institute for Fiscal Studies 1978), Graetz (1980), and Aaron and Galper (1985) all recommended that any capital gain on non-depreciating goods like fine art and jewelry be taxed, even after we have fully transitioned to the consumed-income tax. They all recommended that the capital gain be calculated based on an indexed (i.e., inflation-adjusted) asset basis. I concur but suggest that in this case the capital gain not be eligible for rollover.

18. An exception could be made for any capital loss remaining after a person's entire asset portfolio has been sold off.

19. Proponents of lower taxes on dividends and capital gains argue that this income has already been taxed under the corporate income tax, so the personal income tax on this income constitutes "double taxation." However, if the reforms I will recommend

in chapter 11 are adopted, the corporate income tax would be transformed into a tax on pure, above-normal profits. It would have no disincentive effects whatsoever. There is absolutely nothing wrong with the double, triple, or quadruple taxation of pure excess profits. Hence, this "double taxation" argument for low dividend and capital gains tax rates would become moot.

A similar double taxation argument is often used to suggest that we need corporate tax integration—the combining, through various mechanisms, of the personal income tax with the corporate income tax. Under these reforms only pure excess profits would be double taxed, so there would no need for corporate tax integration either.

Chapter Eight

The Tax Treatment of
Small Businesses

Small businesses, whether sole proprietorships, partnerships, or so-called S corporations, are currently taxed at the individual level. That is, all of the business' income is attributed to its owners, whether the business actually pays that income out or not, and those owners then pay personal income taxes on that income.

Under a consumed-income tax, we want to tax an individual's income only when they consume that income. But any income invested in the business is saved, not consumed. So under a consumed-income tax a business should be treated as it were a traditional IRA: dollars that go in are deductible, earnings that come out are taxed.

Although existing businesses do not currently have the status of IRAs, most of the income they generate for their owners is currently categorized as ordinary earned income, and fully taxable. Similarly, payouts from traditional IRAs are fully taxable. So treating small businesses as if they were IRA-like accounts for the most part makes sense.[1]

EXPENSING NEW CAPITAL INVESTMENT

Moving to a consumed-income tax would only require two modifications to the status quo. The first involves the deduction of the cost of purchasing capital equipment. Under a traditional income tax, whether you purchase equipment or bought a trip to Disney Land doesn't matter—income is income, whether it is consumed (the trip) or adds to your net worth (the equipment). However, once that equipment begins to depreciate, either from wear and tear or by growing obsolete, it loses value. That reduces your net worth. So under the traditional income tax, you are allowed to deduct this loss in value—what economists call "true economic depreciation."

Under a consumed-income tax, we only tax income when it is consumed. So whether you use your income to buy equipment or a trip to Disney Land *does* matter. Buying business equipment is not consuming, so the income used to buy the equipment has effectively been saved. Hence, a consumed-income tax would treat new capital equipment purchases as if they were traditional IRAs: you get an immediate deduction for all the dollars "put in" when purchasing that equipment. We call this immediate tax write-off "asset expensing."

This is another advantage a consumed-income tax has over a traditional income tax. Under the traditional income tax, only true economic depreciation should be deducted. But accurately measuring true economic depreciation is not easy to do. That's partly why we adopted accelerated depreciation in the 1980s. Allowing only true economic depreciation to be deducted required complicated deduction schedules for all kinds of equipment, schedules that needed to be regularly updated. But accelerated depreciation, while simpler, results in inefficient investment decisions.[2]

In contrast, a consumed-income tax calls for asset expensing. You simply deduct the cost of the equipment when you buy it. There's no estimating to be done: if 1,000 different types of equipment have 1,000 different prices, that's no problem, because all the information you need is on your sales receipt. Since all the investment options are treated identically under a consumed-income tax, it's solely the market that drives investment decisions, not the tax code.

There is one downside to asset expensing—any change in the tax rate. Suppose you are a small business owner, currently in the 40% tax bracket. You purchase $10,000 worth of equipment for your business. Immediately deducting that $10,000 would save you $4,000 in taxes. In effect, the government would be putting up 40% of the money needed to buy that equipment. It would then be only appropriate for the government to take a 40% share of the income that equipment generates, no more and no less.[3]

But suppose your tax rate were to change, either because you moved into a different tax bracket or because Congress changed the tax code. You would then be paying some different percent of your business earnings to the government. One way to resolve that problem would be to spread out your $10,000 deduction over the life of the asset, much as we do now with depreciation allowances. Then, if your tax rate were to change, so would the tax savings you got from the deductions.

All of this can be achieved by carrying forward the undepreciated value of the asset *with interest*.[4] I will show you how this would work, but first, a little investment theory.

The rate of return an investor earns on an investment can be broken down into five components. The first is compensation for waiting. If I have $10,000 that I could spend today, but I save and invest it instead, not consuming it until next year, then it is only right that I be compensated for delaying my consumption for a year. Typically, this compensation for waiting pays a rate of return of 1-to-3%.

The second component is a compensation for inflation. If the price level rises by 2%, the goods that your $10,000 could have bought today will cost $10,200 next year. So you need to earn an additional 2% rate of return to offset that 2% inflation.[5]

Together, the compensation for waiting and the compensation for inflation make up the risk-free rate of return. This rate of return is fairly easy to observe, as the rate of return earned on one-year U.S. Treasury bills. Over the last 25 years this rate of return has varied from as low as 0.1% to as high as 7.2%, as economic conditions and inflation expectations have varied. For the purposes of my example, I'll assume that the risk-free rate of return is exactly 5%.[6]

The third and fourth components reflect the riskiness of an investment. They are the risky return and the compensation for bearing risk. Suppose you know you can earn a 5% rate of return, risk free. You're offered an investment opportunity that, half the time, will only pay your original investment back to you, yielding a 0% rate of return. How high would the return have to be, the other half of the time, to make you willing to invest? Let's suppose you answered 20%. Then on average, you would need to earn a 10% rate of return—half of 0% plus half of 20%—to make this investment. Since that is 5% more than the risk-free rate of return, I would conclude that you require that extra 5% compensation to be willing to bear the risk of that plus-or-minus 10% swing in your rate of return.

Most small businesses involve risk. So we would expect the return on an investment made by the small business owner to, on average, earn the risk-free rate of return, plus some compensation for bearing that risk. The actual return earned would then be either higher or lower than this average rate of return, depending on how market conditions actually played out.

Together, these first four components are the normal return to investment, the risky return most investors expect to earn. The fifth and final component to the rate of return is any infra-marginal return. As we saw in chapter 5, an infra-marginal return is the rare result from some unique investment opportunity that yields unexpectedly high returns, or "excess profits." Such returns are extremely rare among small businesses, and would be taxed the same regardless of how we expense or depreciate the asset. Therefore, in this chapter I will assume that there are no infra-marginal returns to worry about.

Suppose you are a small business-person with two, equally attractive investment opportunities. You can buy $10,000 worth of equipment that will yield a guaranteed, risk-free rate of return of 5%, or a different $10,000 worth of equipment that will yield a 0% return half the time, and a 20% return the other half the time. Your tax rate is 40%. Table 8.1 depicts these two investment options under three different depreciation scenarios. It assumes that the investment is made in year 1, and the return occurs in year 2 (at which point the equipment dies).

Table 8.1. The Depreciation Options

Safe Investment		Expensing	Income Tax	Deprec w/Int.
Yr 1	Outlay	$10,000	$10,000	$10,000
	Expensed	$10,000	$0	$0
	Tax Savings	$4,000	$0	$0
	Net Cost	$6,000	$10,000	$10,000
Yr 2	Earnings	$10,500	$10,500	$10,500
	Depreciation	$0	$10,000	$10,500
	Taxable Income	$10,500	$500	$0
	Taxes	$4,200	$200	$0
	After Tax Income	$6,300	$10,300	$10,500
	Rate of Return	5%	3%	5%
Risky Investment (+)		**Expensing**	**Income Tax**	**Deprec w/Int.**
Yr 1	Outlay	$10,000	$10,000	$10,000
	Expensed	$10,000	$0	$0
	Tax Savings	$4,000	$0	$0
	Net Cost	$6,000	$10,000	$10,000
Yr 2	Earnings	$12,000	$12,000	$12,000
	Depreciation	$0	$10,000	$10,500
	Taxable Income	$12,000	$2,000	$1,500
	Taxes	$4,800	$800	$600
	After Tax Income	$7,200	$11,200	$11,400
	Rate of Return	20%	12%	14%
Risky Investment (−)		**Expensing**	**Income Tax**	**Deprec w/Int.**
Yr 1	Outlay	$10,000	$10,000	$10,000
	Expensed	$10,000	$0	$0
	Tax Savings	$4,000	$0	$0
	Net Cost	$6,000	$10,000	$10,000
Yr 2	Earnings	$10,000	$10,000	$10,000
	Depreciation	$0	$10,000	$10,500
	Taxable Income	$10,000	$0	−$500
	Taxes	$4,000	$0	−$200
	After Tax Income	$6,000	$10,000	$10,200
	Rate of Return	0%	0%	2%

With expensing (the first column of numbers), the cost of the equipment is deducted in year 1, reducing its after-tax cost to $6,000. All of the investment's earning are also taxed at the 40% rate. As the table shows, the various rates of return on the business owner's $6,000 stake are all unaffected by the tax—the risk free rate of 5%, the after-tax compensation for bearing risk of 5% (measured by averaging the 20% and 0% rates of return and subtracting the 5% risk free rate of return), and the risk itself (of plus or minus 10%).[7]

Under the traditional income tax (the second column of numbers), the depreciation on the equipment can be deducted in year 2, when the equipment completely wears out. All of the other earnings—that is, all the components of the rate of return—are then taxable. With a 40% tax rate, the after-tax risk-free return is reduced from 5% down to 3%. The after-tax compensation for bearing risk is also reduced to 3% (the average of 12% and 0%, minus the risk free 3%), and the amount of risk falls to plus/minus 6%. Thus, under a 40% traditional income tax the government absorbs 40% of the entire rate of return, including its risky component.

Allowing depreciation to be carried forward with interest (the third column of numbers), at the 5% risk-free interest rate, changes that result. The depreciation deducted in year 2 is increased 5%, to $10,500. Notice that with the risk-free investment, that cancels out all the tax liability: allowing depreciation to be carried forward at the risk-free interest rate leaves the risk-free rate of return untaxed. The compensation for bearing risk is reduced 40%, down to 3% (the average of 14% and 2%, minus the risk free 5%), but the amount of risk is also reduced 40%, to plus/minus 6%.

Allowing depreciation to be carried forward with interest leaves any risk-free investment unaffected by the tax—the same as with expensing. It taxes the risky return to an investment, with the government absorbing both a share of the risk and an equivalent share of the compensation for risk bearing. Hence, allowing depreciation to be carried forward with interest results in the government being a silent partner only in the risky portion of the rate of return.[8]

Under a consumed-income tax businesses could be allowed to choose either to expense their investments, or to depreciate them over their lifetimes. Depreciation allowances would be carried forward at the 1-year Treasury rate of return. The depreciation option is more complicated. But it may be an attractive choice for business owners who either wish to reduce their market risk exposure, or who want to ensure that if tax rates go up, the value of their depreciation allowances rise accordingly.

Fortunately, the benefits of carrying allowances forward with interest does not depend on the rate at which the depreciation allowances are taken. If depreciation allowances are carried forward with interest, a firm that takes its allowances more quickly would still have its risk-free return untaxed. But it would have less of its risk and compensation for risk absorbed by the government. Slowing down the rate that depreciation is taken would have the same impact in reverse. We could easily retain the same depreciation schedules we currently have, and allow firms to choose any combination of expensing/depreciation over time with interest, as long as the assets are fully depreciated over their useful lives. My guess is, most businesses would opt for simplicity, that is, full, immediate expensing. But there would be no harm in giving them the choice.

BUSINESS LOANS

The second modification to the status quo would involve the treatment of business loans. Under a traditional income tax, interest payments are a cost of generating income, so they are deductible. Otherwise, taking out a business loan has no tax consequences.

The logic for a consumed-income tax is very different. As we saw in chapter 5, consumer loans could be treated as taxable—the loan proceeds are taxed, and the loan repayments (principle and interest) are deductible. Or they could be treated as nontaxable—no tax on the loan proceeds are taxed, and no deduction of the loan repayments.

Clearly the taxable treatment of debt makes sense for a small business. Consider a company that currently has $50,000 in business income. If the firm faces a 40% tax rate, it would currently owe $20,000 in taxes.

Suppose the company were to invest in a $200,000 piece of equipment, borrowing $150,000 and using its business income for the other $50,000.[9] If the investment were expensed and the debt were given taxable treatment, the firm would (a) immediately deduct the $200,000 equipment purchase, but (b) be immediately taxed on the $150,000 loan. The net result would be a $50,000 deduction, matching the amount of company income it put into the new investment (table 8.2). That deduction would immediately reduce the firm's taxes by $20,000, to zero.

The investment then generates a profit the next year. With the taxable treatment of debt, the $165,000 paid to the bank (the $150,000 principle plus 10% interest) would be deducted from those profits. The firm would pay taxes only on the $85,000 in net income kept by the business owners (table 8.2).

Just as with consumer loans, the nontaxable treatment of business loans would also be a reasonable alternative. As we saw in table 5.6, a consumer who uses a nontaxable loan to finance an IRA deposit would gain no advantage from delaying their tax payment. This is because the delayed tax pay-

Table 8.2.　Two Treatments of Business Debt

Year 1	Taxable Debt	Nontaxable Debt	Tax Loss Carried Forward
Investment	$200,000	$200,000	$200,000
Firm Equity	$50,000	$50,000	$50,000
Business Loan	$150,000	$150,000	$150,000
Year 2			
Investment Income	$250,000	$250,000	$250,000
Loan Repayment	–$165,000	–$165,000	–$165,000
Net Income	$85,000	$85,000	$85,000
Year 1 Taxable Income			
Other Income	$50,000	$50,000	$50,000
Expensing	–$200,000	-$200,000	–$50,000
Loan Proceeds	$150,000		
Net Income	$0	–$150,000	$0
Tax (40% Tax Rate)	$0	–$60,000	$0
Year 2 Taxable Income			
Investment Income	$250,000	$250,000	$250,000
Depreciation			–$157,500
Loan Repayment	–$165,000		
Net Income	$85,000	$250,000	$92,500
Tax (40% Tax Rate)	$34,000	$100,000	$37,000

ment would have to be repaid with interest when the loan is repaid. That same story applies here. Just as the IRA treatment of savings makes the government a "silent partner" in the investment, the nontaxable treatment of a business loan makes the government a "silent co-lender."

This is also illustrated in table 8.2. With the nontaxable tax treatment, the original $150,000 loan would not be taxed. So expensing the investment would result in a $200,000 first year deduction and a first year tax savings of $80,000. Taxes owed would fall from the original $20,000 down to –$60,000. When the loan is repaid, there would be no repayment deduction, so the full $250,000 in investment income would be taxed. Notice that switching from the taxable treatment of the loan to the nontaxable treatment reduces the firm's taxes in the first year by $60,000, but raises its taxes in the second year by $66,000. In the nontaxable case the government is lending the firm $60,000 in the first year, and then collecting it back at the same 10% interest rate that the bank charged.

In theory, either of these two treatments of business debt would be appropriate under a consumed-income tax. However, the taxable treatment could be open to abuse. With the taxable treatment, the higher the interest payment, the larger the tax deduction. Suppose the borrower and lender were linked—say, two different businesses with the same owners, but one located offshore. An artificially high interest rate would allow the owner to move taxable income from the domestic business to the offshore business, thereby avoiding taxes. Thus, I would recommend that only the nontaxable treatment of debt be allowed.[10]

TAX LOSSES

Our current tax system limits the extent to which small businesses can report tax losses. The reasoning is simple: we don't want people to deduct the costs of their hobbies, which typically don't generate income. Real businesses, on the other hand, should earn incomes that exceeds costs, at least most years. So limiting the deduction of costs to the amount of income earned is a reasonable objective.

The rules for deducting tax losses are necessarily complicated, but they are equally applicable regardless of the type of tax system we adopt. For this section, to keep things simple, I will assume that we are looking at a small business that is unable to deduct any of the tax losses it might incur.

Let me first note that a tax loss does not imply the business is losing money. It only means the business has more tax deductions than it has income. In table 8.2, the business with nontaxable debt had $50,000 in taxable income in year 1, but had $200,000 in deductions from expensing its investment. Thus, it had a tax loss of $150,000.

We saw in an earlier section that there is a reasonable alternative to expensing: depreciation carried forward with interest. Rather than expense the entire $200,000 in year 1, our business could depreciate $50,000 the first year, and depreciate the remaining $150,000 plus $7,500 (the 5% risk free interest rate) in the second year. The results are in the final column of table 8.2.

As you can see from the table, the result is that the small business pays a little bit more in taxes than in the taxable debt scenario. That is because with the nontaxable debt, the government is lending to the business at the bank interest rate of 10%. This interest rate presumably reflects the risk that the business loan will not be repaid. However, the depreciation carried forward only earns the risk-free 5% interest rate. Hence in the final column the government is absorbing some of the firm's risk, but also some of its compensation for risk, which is not occurring in the taxable debt column.

There may be cases where tax losses are not due to expensing, and thus cannot be resolved by moving the depreciation allowances forward with interest. Thus, as a general rule, tax losses should be carried forward with interest. The appropriate interest rate would once again be the market interest rate on a 1-year T bill.[11]

CASH BALANCES

Small businesses should be allowed to hold a reasonable level of cash balances in Roth-IRA eligible assets (up to some limit, perhaps related to the firm's average sales revenue over the previous three years, or the total value of the firm's assets).[12] These balances would not count against the Roth-IRA limits of the businesses owners, unless they exceeded the business' cash balance limit.

Although the assets would be limited to Roth-IRA eligible assets, the business IRA account would otherwise work like a traditional IRA. If retained business earnings were deposited into the account, those earnings would not be taxed, since they had not been withdrawn from the firm. If they were then drawn down to finance a purchase or to cover a payroll, that amount would then be non-deductible, since the deduction for the outlay would be offset by the tax on the IRA withdrawal.

The owners of the business could infuse funds into these cash balance accounts through either an IRA transfer, or a deposit of their other income or wealth into the business IRA. In the latter case, the deposit would count against their annual $50,000 cap.

TRANSITION ISSUES

As usual, there are transition issues. Existing small businesses have assets that have not been expensed, but rather have deductible depreciation allowances. They also have outstanding loans, the interest on which is currently deductible. In the spirit of "taxing the income from old wealth as much as possible under current income tax rules," both of these should be grandfathered in, allowing firms to continue to deduct the depreciation allowances for pre-reform assets, and continue to deduct the interest on pre-reform debt, provided the latter is paid off on schedule.

Another transition issue involves the sale/purchase of a business. Under current law, that sale is actually seen as not one sale, but many: the sale of the buildings and equipment, the sale of any inventory, the sale of the business' name and reputation, the sale of any customer lists, and so on. Some of these individual sales result in ordinary income, some in capital gains income, and some in a combination of ordinary and capital gains income.

For old assets—those acquired under the old tax rules—the tax treatment of their sales would be under the old tax rules, so any capital gains would continue to be taxed as capital gains. Since the tax rates on capital gains and ordinary income would be the same, that distinction would no longer matter.

During the transition, some of those assets wouldn't be fully depreciated for tax purposes. As a result, part of the sale proceeds would be counted as income, but part would be counted as the purchase of the undepreciated value of those assets. The latter would not be taxable income—so it could not be rolled over into a traditional IRA. Rather, it would be counted as the return to the owner of some of his old wealth, in cash form. It too could be deposited into a traditional IRA, but would be subject to the $50,000 limit.

Correspondingly, the purchaser of the business would be allowed to continue to depreciate those old assets, but would also be allowed to expense any assets that had previously been either expensed under the new rules or fully depreciated under the old. It is important to treat the seller and buyer identically for tax purposes. Otherwise, some type of market would arise, that would allow businesses to sell their assets to investors and then lease them back, allowing the business and investor to share in the resulting favorable tax treatment.[13]

All the sale proceeds from any assets expensed under the new tax rules, or fully depreciated under the old tax rules, could be deposited in an IRA on the sale of the business. Those proceeds would be fully taxed if not moved into an IRA. The buyer could expense the entire purchase price, or depreciate the purchased assets over time, with the undepreciated value carried forward at the risk-free interest rate. Once the transition is completed, this would greatly simplify the tax code. The seller would no longer need to distinguish between the different classes of assets and the varying amounts of ordinary and capital gains income. Once the entire business becomes an IRA asset, a withdrawal is a withdrawal, no matter what the form.[14]

ELIMINATING OTHER INCONSISTENCIES

Any tax levied in part or entirely on consumption has the problem of distinguishing between legitimate business costs and outlays that are just personal consumption. Thus, a sales tax, a value added tax, a flat tax, a traditional income tax (which taxes consumption plus gains in net worth), or a consumed-income tax (which taxes consumption, including gains in net worth when those gains are consumed) all have this problem. We have all heard stories about people who go to lunch and pretend to talk business for a minute or two, so they can write off the cost of the lunch as a business expense.

That is a particularly large problem with any progressive income tax, whether a traditional income tax or consumed-income tax. Those who have the highest incomes will typically have the greatest opportunities to deduct legitimate business costs. Being in the highest tax brackets, they have the greatest temptation to deduct outlays that are not really legitimate business expenses.

To reduce the incidence of this tax cheating, we need to tighten the rules on what can and cannot be deducted. The first step would be to eliminate the deductibility of most of the activities that, in a non-business setting, are primarily recreational. Those would include golf memberships or outings, cruises, tickets to sporting events, and of course, restaurant meals.[15]

I have never understood the logic of allowing a deduction for a business lunch. Most people eat lunch, every day, on their own dime. Many people hold business meetings at all times of the day. The mere fact that the two coincide doesn't mean that the food eaten is no longer consumption. And if our goal is to tax consumed income, we should tax all consumed income, no matter what the circumstances.

And yes, if you hadn't been meeting for lunch, maybe you wouldn't have been eating at Chez Maison du Fromage. But if you didn't get a tax break for eating at Chez Maison du Fromage with another business person, you probably wouldn't have been eating there either. Not that there's anything wrong with eating at fancy expensive restaurants. I like to eat at fancy expensive restaurants. But that's the point. It's consumption, and under any consumption-related tax, it should be taxed. Otherwise, we are creating an inefficiency, by encouraging people to satisfy their preferences, not in the lowest cost way, but in the lowest taxed way.

And yes, doctors and salesmen and lawyers and professors and lots of other people need to meet periodically, and conventions are an efficient way to organize those meetings. But conventions, depending on the number of participants, can be held in Chattanooga or Des Moines, in Buffalo or Tucson, in Boston or Atlanta or LA. A convention in Rio or Tahiti or Cancun might be great, but it's no longer just an efficient way to organize meetings. It's a vacation, and that's consumption, which should not be tax deductible.

This is the one place where a consumed-income tax requires us to add to the complexity of our tax code. But it's not because the switch to a consumed-income tax opens up this arena for abuse. The abuse already exists. Rather, the switch to a consumed-income tax makes this abuse all the more intolerable.

In summary, the tax code changes I recommend for small businesses are:[16]

1. Expense new capital investment:
   - Allow new capital equipment to be immediately and fully expensed (or depreciated over its lifetime, with the undepreciated value carried forward at the risk-free interest rate).

2. Give business debt nontaxable treatment:
   • Eliminate the interest deduction for new business debt.
3. Limit Roth IRAs to low risk investments:
   • Allow small businesses to hold cash balances (up to some limit) in Roth-IRA accounts.
4. Eliminate special tax treatments:
   • Tighten the rules on the deduction of "business" consumption.
5. Transition rules:
   • Allow the continued deductible depreciation of business assets purchased before the tax change;
   • Allow the continued deduction of interest on old business loans, provided they continue to be paid off in a timely fashion;
   • Allow the portion of the sale of a business taxed as ordinary income to be rolled over into an IRA;
   • Allow the purchaser of a business to expense the portion of the sale of a business taxed as ordinary income for the seller.
6. Other:
   • Allow tax losses to be carried forward at the risk-free interest rate.

NOTES

1. It may appear that this provides more favorable tax treatment to those who hold their old wealth in the form of business assets than to those who hold their old wealth in the form of stocks and bonds. However, stockowners can already shelter much of their capital income from immediate taxation by delaying their realization of capital gains; business owners currently have no such option.

I would also note that on average the owners of stocks and bonds are wealthier than the owners of business assets. According to Saez and Zucman (2015, Appendix Tables(Distributions)), in 2012 the wealthiest 1% of the U.S. population held about 69% of all U.S. stock (equity) wealth, but only 44% of all U.S. business assets. At the very top of the wealth distribution, the wealthiest 0.01% of the U.S. population held about 24.6% of all stock (equity) wealth, but only 7.6% of all business assets.

2. Gravelle (2001) discusses these issues in depth.

3. The 40% tax rate will be used throughout this chapter, because it provides relatively easy-to-follow round numbers for the illustrations. In reality, for most realistically progressive tax systems, only the highest-earning small businesses would face that high of a tax rate.

4. Boadway and Bruce (1984).

5. Over the last 30 years, inflation has averaged just over 2.5%. The Federal Reserve currently sets its inflation target at around 2%.

6. Technically, even one-year U.S. Treasuries are not risk-free. Although the likelihood that the Federal government will default is roughly zero, Treasuries do carry

the risk that actual inflation will differ from the expected inflation rate. However, they are the best measure of the risk-free rate of return available.

7. If the business owner is earning just a normal rate of return—that is, no infra-marginal profits—then his or her initial $4,000 tax savings from the equipment purchase can be reinvested in some other risk-free or risky investment, also earning those same rates of return. This reinvestment activity can continue until the business owner is earning those rates of return on his or her full $10,000. This effectively cancels out the fact that the government, through expensing, is a silent 40% partner in each of those investment ventures.

8. One can argue that investors can easily offset this silent partner arrangement by choosing more risky investments. Although this argument makes a lot of sense for people investing in say the stock market, I doubt that it applies to small business owners, whose level of risk might be baked into the nature of their business itself.

9. This $50,000 is called "firm equity."

10. Both the Hall and Rabushka (1995) flat tax and David Bradford's (2005) X-tax would also ignore loans altogether, effectively providing them nontaxable treatment.

11. Aaron and Galper (1985, 83) proposed that losses be carried forward with interest, as part of their cash flow tax proposal. Similarly, Hall and Rabushka (1995, 64), in their flat tax proposal, proposed that loss balances carried forward "will earn the market rate of interest." It is clear from their examples—a 6% interest rate for 1995, a 14% interest rate in their first edition for 1981—that they meant using the nominal interest rate on short-term Treasury bills.

The President's Advisory Panel (2005) also recommended providing interest on loss carry-forwards; however their example, which began with the phrase "if the current interest rate is 10 percent," suggests that they were envisioning a risk-adjusted interest rate. Similarly Keuschnigg and Keuschnigg (2012), in examining tax transitions, state that "the [tax] system would only be approximately neutral if the carry-forward interest rate were not equal to the firm's discount rate." Carroll and Viard (2012) initially proposed carry-forwards with interest at the rate on short-term Treasuries, but in a footnote suggest allowing firms to pre-elect some risky rate, like the return on the stock market.

Using the logic developed in the earlier section of this chapter, carrying losses forward using some risk-adjusted interest rate would leave the business' compensation for bearing risk untaxed. Since the government, through the tax system, would be absorbing a share of the risk itself, it seems more appropriate for the government also to be taking a share of that compensation as well. Further, trying to use the firm's discount rate—that is, the risk-adjusted interest rate appropriate to the level of risk the firm faces—would create insurmountable measurement problems. Nor is the return on the stock market a reasonable proxy, since individual business risk is at best only imperfectly correlated with aggregate market risk.

12. This might be particularly useful for partnerships, where the ownership of the cash account would be divided among several partners.

13. To the extent that some of the undepreciated assets are valued in the sale at more than their depreciated value, subjecting the seller to "recapture" on that depreciation, which is taxed as ordinary income, that excess depreciation could be expensed

by the purchaser. Thus, all taxable-income proceeds from the sale for the seller would be immediately deductible costs for the buyer, and any nontaxable proceeds for the seller would be depreciable assets for the buyer.

14. If the business owner had chosen to gradually depreciate the new assets under the new tax rules, the remaining undepreciated value could be completely depreciated at the time of the sale.

15. Halperin (1974) provides a comprehensive analysis of these issues. In general, I agree with his recommendations (932).

16. Although this book focuses primarily on reforming the individual income tax, these same changes—expensing new investment, and treating new debt as either fully taxable or nontaxable—would also clean up many of the problems associated with the corporate income tax. This will be discussed further in chapter 11.

Chapter Nine

Inheritances, Bequests, and the Estate Tax

In chapter 1, I defined a consumed-income tax as a tax on all income, levied not in the year that the income is earned, but rather in the year that it is consumed. That definition works fairly well for most of us, since most of us eventually consume most of the income that we ever earn. But then again it doesn't quite work perfectly for most of us. For the extremely rich, who earn much more in their lifetimes than they can possibly consume, it doesn't work at all. So if the goal is to tax all income when it is consumed, how should we handle the income that doesn't get consumed? That is, how should we handle estates, bequests, and the resulting inheritances?

We currently handle this issue by levying an estate tax, sometimes called the "death tax" by its opponents, on estate bequests. As we'll see, switching from the traditional income tax logic to a consumed-income tax logic does not entirely eliminate the controversy that surrounds the estate tax. But it will clarify it, and give us a cleaner conceptual background for determining whether estates should or shouldn't be taxed.

INHERITANCES

First though, let me make an observation that should not be controversial. If our goal is to tax consumed income, and put the highest tax rates on those who consume most lavishly, then inheritances should be treated as taxable income. If my Uncle Larry leaves me $10 million, then I've received income.[1] If I immediately squander that income on babes, booze, and bling, well, that's consumed income, so it's only fair that the taxman takes a big bite out of my windfall. On the other hand, if I deposit most of my windfall into a traditional

IRA, and only consume a modest proportion of my inheritance each year, I should only be taxed modestly, as my inherited income is consumed. This implies that the entire inheritance should be eligible to be sheltered in an IRA, above and beyond the normal $50,000 limitation.

Taxing the accumulated capital gain on inherited assets would no longer be an issue, as it is under the current tax law. It doesn't matter what Uncle Larry paid for his stock portfolio. Anything you inherit and then immediately sell and spend would be immediately taxed. Similarly, anything you inherit and then eventually sell and spend would also be taxed, but only eventually.

Notice that if you inherit Grandma's IRA, and don't withdraw anything from it, you'll have no immediate tax liability. That's dramatically simpler than how we currently tax inherited IRAs. Under a traditional income tax, an IRA is an anomaly: income that should have been taxed when it was earned, but wasn't. That's why, under our current system, Grandma must take required withdrawals from her IRA once she hits 70. But often, the IRA isn't entirely emptied before Grandma dies. So under current law, if you inherit some of her IRA, you must make withdrawals from it every year until it is emptied, beginning in the year you inherit it.

In contrast, under a consumed-income tax, delaying taxes until the income is consumed makes perfect sense. So if Grandma never got around to consuming the last bit of her IRA savings, and passed some of it on to you, you won't be taxed on it until you choose to withdraw the savings and consume it.

Similarly, if you inherit the family business and sell it, the sale proceeds would be taxable. But if you continue to operate it, you would have no immediate tax liability. All of the assets you inherited were left in the business—effectively, in an IRA-like account—and only your withdrawals will be taxable.[2]

In the previous three paragraphs I implicitly assumed that your inheritance came in the form of cash or financial assets like stocks or bonds or a business. But what if you inherit consumer goods, like a house or car or furniture? For most of us, that includes only a few household goods with sentimental value: Grandma's best china or Dad's golf clubs. Simplicity suggests that we dispense with taxing these goods, by giving everyone a lifetime $10,000 exemption on inherited household goods.

Houses and other high-value goods, like fine art, present a more difficult challenge (unless the heirs decide to sell them). Taxing them in one lump sum might throw the heir into a higher tax bracket. It could also create a cash-flow problem, forcing the heirs to sell off these assets against their preferences. To solve this, imagine the heirs (a) sold the house, and put the funds into an IRA, cancelling out the tax liability; (b) repurchased the house at the same price; (c) paid for that repurchase with a 30-year 5% mortgage for the house's full value; and (d) paid off the mortgage over the next 30 years by making withdrawals from the IRA. Then they would only owe taxes on the IRA withdrawals over the next 30 years.

We can mimic that tax treatment, without all the complexity, by requiring the heirs to pay taxes on 6.2% of the house's inherited value for the next 30 years (counting the inheritance year as Year 1 of the 30).[3] Alternatively, the heir could choose to pay taxes on 7.65% of the house's inherited value for the next 20 years, or on 9.2% of the house's inherited value for the next 15 years. All three tax treatments would allow individuals to pay off the tax liability over a reasonable amount of time, while earning the government roughly 5% interest on the delayed tax payments.

Taxing inheritances has the side benefit of transitioning old wealth into the framework of the consumed-income tax. Grandpa the billionaire may have tons of money stuck outside of IRAs, but when he passes this wealth on to the next generation, they will put it all into IRAs until they are ready to spend it. It may take quite a while, but eventually all non-business assets end up in IRAs.

BEQUESTS

So, inheritances should be treated as taxable income, with the entire inheritance IRA-eligible. So what does that say about the bequest? Uncle Larry earned $50 million over his lifetime, and spent $40 million of it. Then he died, leaving me the rest. Should he—or more precisely, his estate—be taxed on that other $10 million?

Opponents of an estate tax argue that since the income has not yet been consumed, it should not yet be taxed. Sure, when I get my hands on Uncle Larry's money and blow it in wild revelry, *I* should get taxed. But Uncle Larry never spent it, so his estate should owe the government nothing.[4] This perspective is consistent with the idea of a consumption tax, like a sales tax, which taxes all consumption, but only consumption. But a consumed-income tax taxes all income. Consumption is only the signal for when that income should be taxed. So it is *not* consistent with the logic of consumed-income tax to leave Uncle Larry's unspent income untaxed.[5]

It can be argued that a consumed-income tax is fairer than a traditional income tax, because it treats people with the same lifetime opportunities more equally. Suppose that over our lifetimes, you and I both earn the exact same paychecks, giving us the exact same lifetime spending opportunities. Suppose that I take advantage of those opportunities by spending every penny I earn, the year I earn it, saving nothing whatsoever. You however are less like Aesop's grasshopper and more like his ant, putting aside a bit of each paycheck for your future needs.

A traditional income tax would tax you more than me over our lifetimes, since it would include any interest you earned from your savings in the tax base. A consumed-income tax would tax us equally: since it has a zero effective tax rate on that interest, we would both be taxed just on our lifetime paycheck earnings, which are identical. So from this lifetime-opportunities perspective, the consumed-income tax is fairer than a traditional income tax.[6]

Now, perhaps you agree with this way of defining fairness, and perhaps you don't. After all, fairness, like beauty, is in the eye of the beholder. However, you must admit that it's at least a reasonable way to define a fair tax system. From this perspective, some of us may choose to spend those opportunities more immediately, and some of us may choose to delay our consumption somewhat. But if we all have the same opportunities, then it's not entirely unreasonable to say that we all have the same ability to pay taxes.

Many of the advocates for consumption-timed taxes accept this fairness viewpoint. But if you accept this perspective, you should also accept the need for an estate tax. After all, suppose that Grasshopper and Ant have the same opportunity to consume over their lifetimes, but while Grasshopper uses that opportunity to spend all of his resources over his lifetime, Ant only spends most of her resources, leaving the rest to her heirs. Ant and Grasshopper will only be taxed equally on their equal opportunities if Ant's estate is taxed on the opportunities that she never consumed.[7]

Again, a consumed-income tax, like a traditional income tax, attempts to tax all income. Uncle Larry paid taxes on the $40 million of his income that he spent. But he never paid taxes on the remaining $10 million. So now, when his assets are passed on to me, that tax is due.[8]

Opponents of the estate tax sometimes claim that this argument misstates the issue. The fairness question, they say, should be framed as one of multigenerational families. The opportunities of me and my heirs, they argue, should be compared to the opportunities of you and your heirs. If one of us shares our consumption opportunities with their heirs and the other doesn't, the first family gets taxed extra, because the shared earnings are taxed both when they are bequeathed and when they are spent by some future generation. I find this viewpoint interesting, but not at all convincing. Under what other circumstance do we define fairness in a way that involves multiple generations?

Besides, the story has to be one where the spending opportunities of these two multigenerational families are the same. Each family must be earning the exact same amount of labor income in each generation. That is, the grandparents in families A and B have the same lifetime labor income, and their children have the same lifetime labor income, and so on. But suppose that is the case, and Grandparents A leave their children a bequest that Grandparents B don't leave their children. Don't the children in Family A have greater lifetime spending opportunities than their Family B counterparts?

Hence, if there are differences in bequests, we can either have equality in opportunity for the individual family members, or equality in opportunity for the multigenerational families, but not both. And in my mind, the concept of treating individuals fairly seems the far more cogent concept.

There's an entirely different way to look at the question of whether estates should be taxed under a consumed-income tax. Let me introduce this other viewpoint with two anecdotes.

A number of years ago, the director of a prominent Omaha hospital got a late night phone call. A man had been admitted into the hospital with chest pains, and was requesting a private room. But the man didn't have health insurance, and the hospital had a policy of only allowing private rooms for patients with health insurance. What, the people in admissions asked, should they do?

The next day, the hospital's policy was formally amended. From then on, private rooms were only available to those who were either insured, or rich enough to be able to buy the entire hospital with their spare change. That is to say, if the patient were Warren Buffett.

Now, I don't really know if this story has any truth to it or not. But it is believable. After all, why would Warren Buffett need to buy health insurance? I have health insurance to cover any major medical expense that might arise. Without insurance, getting hit with cancer or something of the like might bankrupt me. But there is no medical emergency that Warren Buffett couldn't handle financially. So why on earth would he bother to buy health insurance?

The second anecdote involves me. I'm a retired University professor, with a state pension and social security income that provides me with a reasonably comfortable living. I also have a nice-sized retirement savings account that I've built up over the years. It's nothing that would impress Warren Buffett, but if I or my wife should eventually need home care or hospice, we'll be able to afford it without becoming a burden on our children.

With my pension and social security check, I have no need to consume any of my IRA savings. But as my anecdote suggests, I do get an ongoing consumption benefit from that wealth, a freedom from worry about what may happen to my wife and me in our last years. Likewise, Warren Buffett gets consumption benefits from his wealth, even without spending it. Warren Buffett is renowned for being enormously wealthy yet living a simple, almost Spartan lifestyle. Is he better off than the guy down the street who can barely afford that same simple lifestyle? Certainly Warren doesn't have to worry about outliving his wealth, the way his neighbor does. So yes, owning wealth provides the owner with consumption benefits that should be taxed.[9]

Indeed, the world of finance gives us a very precise way to at least imagine how we might measure these consumption benefits. Warren Buffett holds an option, an option to increase his consumption dramatically, or to maintain his current consumption even if his income were to disappear. This option is not unlike many of the financial options that Mr. Buffett also holds, "put" and "call" options that allow him to buy or sell stock at some predetermined price, the same kinds of stock options that corporate executives are often given.

Options have value. Financial options are regularly bought and sold at observable market prices. Individuals and businesses pay money to own them. So holding wealth provides a consumption option, and that option has value. Therefore, we could very reasonably interpret that as a type of consumption our consumed-income tax should tax.

Any attempt to tax that "options" consumption during Warren Buffett's lifetime would create all kinds of problems. Those would be the exact same problems that arise with a traditional income tax. So let's not even consider doing that. But we can indirectly tax that consumption after Mr. Buffett dies, by levying an estate tax, that only falls on exceptionally large estates, like Mr. Buffett's.

Herbert Stein, chairman of the Council of Economic Advisors under both Nixon and Ford, once asked how we should tax a person who only spends $40,000 of his $200,000 income. Should he be taxed like someone who spends all of his $40,000 income, asked Stein, or like someone who spends all of his $200,000 income?[10]

Including an estate tax as part of the consumed-income tax ensures that this person will be taxed more than the person who spends all of his $40,000 income, but effectively less than the person who spends all of his $200,000 income. (The estate tax on the unspent income would be delayed for many years, which we saw in chapter 2 implies a lower effective tax rate.) Taxing this person somewhere between these other two individuals seems eminently fair, and eminently appropriate, to me.

Under current law, each individual can pass down to his or her heirs up to about $11.2 million in wealth, tax-free.[11] For a married couple, if the husband dies first, he can pass that amount to his children and the rest to his wife, all tax-free. Then when she dies, another $11.2 million in wealth can be passed down tax-free. Thus, a couple can leave up to about $22.4 million to their children without the estate tax kicking in. As a result, only the wealthiest 0.2 percent of estates—that's 1 in 500—pay the estate tax. These are not the estates of small businessmen or small family farmers. These are the estates of the truly wealthy.[12]

As the author of *Blueprints for Basic Tax Reform* noted, the "equity judgment in present law is that large transfers [of wealth] should be [progressively taxed], and relatively small transfers need not be taxed. This has general appeal."[13] I fully agree. Maintaining an estate tax along the lines of the one in our current tax system is a reasonable balance between simplicity and fairness. It lets the vast majority of gifts and estates go tax-free, further simplicity. It also lets small transfers go tax-free, which is the fair treatment from the multigenerational perspective. But it imposes a tax on large transfers, which is the fair treatment from the individual perspective.

That does not mean the estate tax does not need not to be reformed. It has too many special provisions that allow wealthy families to avoid paying the tax—so many that the Secretary of the Treasury recently suggested that "only fools pay the estate tax." We should make it far more difficult for those extremely wealthy few to avoid supporting the Republic that gave them the opportunity to acquire that great wealth. After all, the people who undergo personal sacrifices to benefit this great nation of ours should not be deemed fools; they should be hailed as patriots.

GIFTS

Most gifts are small—Christmas presents and the like—and ignoring them for tax purposes makes perfect sense. Effectively, if I spend $60 to buy you a sweater, I'm taxed on your consumption, so my gift includes not just the sweater, but the tax liability as well.

There are two exceptions. Under current tax law, gifts that exceed $14,000 a year are taxable, with the tax paid by the giver. We have this provision to prevent the wealthy from making large deathbed gifts to avoid the estate tax. This provision should be kept. In addition, any gifts over $14,000 a year that are received should be treated exactly like inherited income: fully taxable, but also fully IRA-eligible.[14]

INHERITANCES REDUX

I've recommended that we tax both estates (the money left behind by those who die) and inheritances (the money received by their heirs). Isn't this double taxation? And if we tax estates, is there any need to tax inheritances as well?

The answer to the first question is yes, it would be double taxation. But we currently double tax wages and salaries, first by taking out taxes for Social

Security, Medicare, and the like, and then by taking out income taxes. It's not the number of taxes that matter, it's the size of the combined tax. Suppose the estate tax rate stays at 40%, and the top income tax rate were also at 40%. Then $1,000 of taxable estate would be reduced to a $600 inheritance, after the 40% estate tax was collected. This would in turn allow $360 of consumption, after the 40% inheritance tax was collected—so a combined 64% tax rate. Since the estate tax has a roughly $22 million exemption, this 64% tax would only apply to extremely large estates. So yes, I think double taxation would be perfectly appropriate in this case.

Second, we absolutely do need to tax inheritances, even if we retain the estate tax. Recall that the first $22.4 million of an estate avoids the estate tax altogether. So let's look at an example, involving an $8.6 million estate.

John and Mary Lucky were small but savvy investors in the 1980s. John was a computer engineer, so when a small company called Apple Computer first sold its shares publicly in 1980, John decided to buy 400 shares at the offered price of $22 per share, an $8,800 investment. Over the years, these shares split four times, with the original 400 shares turning into 22,400 shares.

In 1986, another computer-related company, called Microsoft, made its initial public offering of shares. Mary suggested that this was also a good bet, and John concurred, so they purchased 200 shares at $21 each. Over the years, these shares split 9 times, with the original 200 shares turning into 57,600 shares.

After they retired, John and Mary lived off of John's retirement, plus their dividends from these two investments, but they never needed to sell any of the shares themselves. So when they died last year, they were able to leave an estate worth $8.4 million: $3.8 million worth of Apple shares, which were selling at $170 each, and $4.6 million worth of Microsoft shares, which were selling at $80 each.

Since their estate was less than $10 million, no estate tax was owed, so their son Dudley inherited the entire $8.4 million stock portfolio. The share prices have remained steady over the last year, still selling at $170 and $80 respectively. So when Dudley sold 560 shares of Apple and 576 shares of Microsoft this year, he got $141,280 for them, which he was able to spend this year, absolutely tax-free.

How was he able to do this? Isn't there an enormous capital gain on all those shares, that Dudley owes taxes on? After all, those 560 shares of Apple were, before all the stock splits, originally just ten shares, which his parents bought for $220. And those 576 shares of Microsoft were, before all those stock splits, originally just two shares, which his parents bought for $42. Doesn't Dudley owe taxes on that $141,016 capital gain that he just realized?

The answer is, under current tax law, no he doesn't. Our current tax law allows the cost basis for the capital gain—the number we count as the original purchase price, and so the untaxed portion of the sale price—to be "stepped up" when the asset is inherited. So Dudley's basis for his stock portfolio is the full $8.4 million that it was worth the day he inherited it. If he were able to sell some of his Apple shares today for say $175 each, he would owe capital gains taxes only on the $5 per share that they'd appreciated after he inherited them.

Most of us get up five days a week, and go to an office, or factory, or store, or whatever else our place of business might be, and put in an honest day's work to earn our paycheck. Under either a traditional or a consumed-income tax, we are taxed on all of that paycheck, either immediately or when we eventually spend it. So it does not seem right to me that Dudley, who only had to be fortunate enough to have John and Mary as his parents, and who can as a result afford to have a somewhat more lavish lifestyle than you or I, can entirely or almost entirely avoid the tax burden that you and I must shoulder.

An inheritance is income. We shouldn't say it's not income just because Dudley never had to work for it. Rather, the fact that Dudley never worked for his money is all the more reason that it should be taxed. And if Dudley is so fortunate that he inherits not $8.4 million, but $28.4 million, taxing all but $10 million twice seems about right to me. So yes, we should tax both estates and inheritances.

In summary, the tax code changes I recommend for inheritances and bequests are:

1. Eliminate special tax treatments:
   • Tax inheritances and large gifts as income.
2. Allow (almost) all new savings to be tax sheltered:
   • Allow inherited cash and financial assets and large financial gifts to be fully deposited into an IRA;
   • Allow previously expensed inherited business assets to be expensed.
3. Transition rules:
   • Allow the continued deductible depreciation of not fully depreciated inherited business assets purchased before the tax change.
4. Other:
   • Allow a lifetime $10,000 exemption on inherited household goods;
   • Allow the tax on inherited consumer durables to be paid over a 30 year period, with interest;
   • Modify the estate tax to reduce tax avoidance.

NOTES

1. Recall the Schanz-Haig-Simon definition of income from chapter 2.

2. More exactly, the inherited business assets would be expensed, with the deduction for expensing the acquired assets offsetting the tax on the inheritance. It is possible, especially immediately after the change in the tax system, that some of the inherited family business' assets will not yet have been fully tax depreciated. A reasonable transition treatment would be to continue to allow depreciation deductions on those assets, until they are fully depreciated. See chapter 7 for other examples of transition treatments.

3. A $6,200 annual payment, starting in the year the mortgage was taken out, would pay off a $100,000 5% mortgage in 30 years.

4. Graetz (1980) took this view. However, he noted that if the increased concentration of wealth is an issue, an estate tax would be appropriate. As Minarek (1985) pointed out, a consumed-income tax would have exactly that effect, increasing the concentration of wealth, unless gifts and bequests were taxed.

5. Aaron and Galper (1985). Incidentally, the same logic applies to income moved abroad. Goode (1980) expressed concern that a person who accumulated a fortune under an expenditure tax could avoid taxation by moving abroad. Aaron and Galper (1985) suggest that deductions for savings only be allowed for deposits into U.S. financial accounts, and a withholding tax be levied on withdrawals going abroad.

6. Musgrave (1976) developed this argument. Keep in mind that this argument is a statement only about horizontal equity, that is, the equal treatment of those who are equally well off. It says nothing about the relative tax treatments of those who are higher or lower on the income scale.

7. Musgrave (1976).

8. Simons (1938) argued that the bequest itself was consumption on the part of the giver, and so should be taxed. Goode (1980) agreed, arguing that this provision is needed so that "the differences between the [traditional] income tax and the expenditure tax . . . would reduce to differences in the timing of tax payments." Mieszkowski (1978) took a similar view, stating that "the taxation of bequests as consumption of the deceased . . . merely fulfill the requirement that a particular household be taxed on the basis of lifetime endowment," as did Stiglitz (1985).

9. As the Meade Committee noted, "wealth itself, quite apart from the income it produces, confers independence, security, and influence" (Institute for Fiscal Studies 1978, 318).

10. Quoted in Graetz (1997, 205).

11. Aaron and Galper (1985) suggested that gifts and estates be taxed, with a lifetime exemption of $100,000 per person. Current law is significantly more generous, even after adjusting their figure for inflation.

12. Prior to the Dec. 2017 Tax Cuts and Jobs Act (TCJA), the limit was $5.6 million per person.

13. Bradford, et al. (1984, 38).

14. The various exceptions to the gift tax, including gifts to finance higher education and gifts to finance medical care, should also be kept.

Chapter Ten

Insurance

It is not immediately obvious how we should classify insurance when we are designing a tax system. Is owning insurance a form of consumption? If I receive an insurance payout, is it income? Should insurance premiums be deductible or not?

These questions are even more problematic when we deal with whole-life and universal-life insurance policies. These policies have a savings element as well as a pure insurance element. They have cash values that build up, which can be used as collateral for a loan. And they have dividends that can be paid out. Our current tax treatment of these types of insurance is not consistent with any particular tax logic, which only compounds the problem.

To explore how we should treat insurance under a consumed-income tax, I will first need to develop a framework for thinking about what insurance does. I will then identify the several different types of insurance. I will look at how each of these should be taxed under a traditional income tax, and compare that to what we currently do. Then I will identify the changes needed to tax insurance coherently under a consumed-income tax.

INSURANCE AS "MOVING CONSUMPTION"

There's a way of looking at insurance that shows its similarities with saving and borrowing. Saving and borrowing can be viewed as "moving consumption between periods of time." Insurance is "moving consumption between risk-states."

Saving and borrowing both move consumption from one time period to another. When you save, you forgo some amount of consumption today. But those savings allow you to consume more in the future. So saving moves some present consumption into the future. Conversely, when you borrow you consume more now, but less later, when you'll have to repay the loan. So borrowing moves some future consumption into the present.

Insurance also moves consumption, but now between different risk outcomes, or "risk-states." Suppose there's a 1% chance of your having an auto accident this year. Then the two "risk-states" are (a) no-accident-occurring (a 99% likelihood) and (b) an-accident-does-occur (a 1% likelihood).

Suppose one year's auto insurance costs $400, but you don't buy insurance. If no accident occurs, you'll have all of your income to spend on consumption. But if an accident does occurs, you'll no longer have your car, so you'll have to divert a large chunk of income to replacing the lost vehicle. By buying insurance, you've reduced your amount available for spending on other things this year by $400. So you've given up $400 worth of consumption in the risk-state where no accident occurs. But also, by buying insurance, you've eliminated the huge loss in consumption in the risk-state where an accident does occur. By buying insurance, you move consumption from the "I-got-lucky-and-no-accident-occurred" risk-state to the "oops-I-was-unlucky" risk-state.

This viewpoint is not particularly helpful when thinking about a traditional income tax. After all, under a traditional income tax, all of this year's income should be taxed, whether I save it or spend it. And if I do save some, the extra interest income I earn next year should be taxed as well. Under a traditional income tax, "moving consumption" can have all kinds of tax consequences.

Under a consumed-income tax however, this viewpoint can be extremely helpful. After all, under a consumed income tax, income is taxed when it is consumed, so when consumption is "moved," so are taxes. Under a consumed-income tax, when I save for tomorrow, I move my consumption from today to tomorrow, so my saved income is taxed tomorrow, not today. The consumed-income tax achieves this by allowing deposits into an IRA to be deducted, and withdrawals from the IRA to be taxed.

Similarly, if I buy insurance, I move my consumption from the low-risk-state to the high-risk-state. In the low-risk-state I have less consumption, so I should be taxed less. This can be achieved by allowing insurance premiums to be deducted. In the high-risk-state, insurance allows me to have more consumption, so I should be taxed more. Therefore I should be taxed on any insurance payouts that I receive.

As we have seen however, under certain circumstances treating saving in exactly the opposite way—not allowing a deduction for the deposits into saving, but not taxing the withdrawals from savings—could also make sense.[1] If the original saved income were taxed when it was earned, the saver would have "prepaid" the tax on his or her future consumption. By a similar logic, we could choose to not tax insurance payouts, but only if we then did not allow a deduction for the insurance premiums.

Either tax approach—deducting insurance premiums and taxing insurance payouts, or not deducting insurance premiums and not taxing insurance payouts—is consistent with the logic of a consumed-income tax.[2] For some forms of insurance, the first approach has distinct advantages. For other forms of insurance, the second approach clearly makes more sense. In most cases, it probably makes no difference which choice we make, as long as we stick to one of the two approaches. In these last cases, my recommendation will be to go for simplicity, which means neither deducting premiums nor taxing payouts.

PROPERTY/LIABILITY INSURANCE

The simplest types of insurance to deal with are property insurance and liability insurance. Property insurance covers the loss of or damage to your own personal property; liability insurance covers any legal liability from injury to other people or damage to their property. Both types of insurance protect you from the loss of your property, either from fire, theft, damage, or legal seizure. Homeowner's insurance, renter's insurance and auto insurance are all examples, as are a variety of business insurances.

Under a traditional income tax, the loss of property is a decrease in net worth, so it should be deductible. Under current law you can take a "casualty loss" deduction for uninsured losses that exceed 10% of your adjusted gross income. If the loss is insured, the insurance payout cancels out the loss in net worth, so there is neither a gain nor loss—and hence no tax consequences either way. This is in fact our current tax treatment of property/casualty insurance, so current law for these types of insurance makes perfect sense under a traditional income tax.[3]

Under a consumed-income tax, when you bought any of these consumer durables—your house, your car, your furniture, and so forth—that purchase was treated as if it were a Roth IRA. The purchase was not deductible, so you in effect prepaid the tax on the stream of consumption that the durable item was going to provide you.

A casualty event—a theft, a fire, whatever—would prematurely cut off this stream of consumption. If this loss is not insured, this is again a loss in net worth for the remaining portion of the consumption stream that you've already paid taxes on. So the taxes on this loss should be refunded to you. Like under the traditional income tax, the uninsured casualty loss should be deductible (but again, only if it exceeds say 10% of AGI).

By purchasing these types of property insurance, you are merely buying the risk free version of the consumer durable. With insurance, your consumer durable will not have its useful life cut short, because if damage occurs, the insurance company will replace it for you. It therefore makes sense to treat this type of insurance like a Roth IRA: no deduction when you purchase it, and no tax on the proceeds if it pays out. Since again this is current tax law, switching to a consumed-income tax requires no changes in how we treat property insurance.[4]

The same logic applies to casualty events that impact others' property. If you have an auto accident, and damage my car, you have prematurely cut off my expected consumption stream which I'd already paid taxes on. Your insurance company's payout to me merely restores my loss, so it should have no tax impact on me.

Usually, property insurance and liability insurance have another component that covers injuries to others. That component can be thought of as partly medical insurance, and partly income protection insurance (protecting the incomes of the others you injure). I'll discuss those in the next two sections.

INCOME PROTECTION INSURANCE

Short-term disability insurance, permanent life insurance, and term life insurance all replace lost income, either due to death (life insurance) or some other catastrophe (disability or income replacement insurance). They ensure that some portion of the income you expect to earn over your working lifetime will continue, even if you can no longer work and earn that income.

Under a traditional income tax, if you die or become disabled, there are no immediate tax consequences, because you are not, as far as the tax code in concerned, considered an asset. So there are no assets lost, and no capital loss to deduct. It's just that the stream of taxable income that would have occurred no longer does.

If you have insurance, some or all of that lost income reappears. That new income—the insurance proceeds—is income by the Schanz-Haig-Simons definition, since the proceeds can finance either consumption or an increase in net worth. So under the logic of a traditional income tax, any proceeds from life or disability insurance should be taxed. Furthermore, any life insurance policies that accrue in value increase the owner's net worth. Under a traditional income tax, those increases, whether paid out or not, should be taxable income as well.

But that is not what our current tax system does. Life insurance proceeds are generally not taxed as income, although they may be taxed under the estate tax. Disability insurance proceeds may or may not be taxed, depending on whether the individual or his employer paid for the insurance. And the "inside buildup" of permanent life insurance goes tax-free.

This is just one more case where moving to a consumed-income tax cleans up something that is messy and complicated under a traditional income tax. Under a consumed-income tax, life and disability insurance just move consumption from the no-accident-happens-state to the accident-occurs-state. By buying life insurance on myself, I give up some consumption if I live; my family gains consumption if I die. Since the payouts are easily observable, and in cash form, the simplest logic is that they should be treated as other forms of inheritance income, that is, taxed. But the life insurance premiums should be deductible.

For permanent life insurance, this would in effect give the saving component of a permanent life insurance policy traditional IRA status: a deduction for dollars in, a tax on dollars out. Once again, taxing correctly is relatively easy, once you adopt the logic of a consumed-income tax.

The same logic applies to disability insurance, except now I'm the one who pays taxes on the insurance payouts that I get if I'm injured. Those payouts provide income I can consume now, and so they should be taxed now, except for any deposited into an IRA.

Notice that this would let us eliminate any tax distinction between employer-financed disability insurance and worker-financed disability insurance. If my employer pays for the insurance while paying me a smaller salary, he gets to deduct the cost of the insurance. If he pays me the somewhat higher salary and I then buy the insurance, I get to deduct the cost of the insurance. Either way, if I'm injured, the insurance proceeds are taxed.[5]

There is once again however an alternative logic, that suggests treating these forms of insurance like Roth IRAs. Most of us are probably somewhat underinsured, so to increase our protection against the hazards of death and disability, it could make sense to move some of our tax liabilities from the "something-bad-happened" state to the "whew-everything-is-still-good" state. That could be achieved by *not* allowing a deduction for the insurance premiums, and *not* taxing the insurance payouts. Those who don't get injured will pay a little more in taxes, while those who receive the payout will get them tax-free. The result is effectively a bit more insurance, automatically purchased from Uncle Sam.

This Roth-like treatment would effectively treat the savings component of permanent life insurance as a Roth IRA: no deduction for deposits, no tax on withdrawals. Life insurance policies that build up value are already heavily regulated, and so would meet the Roth "low risk" restriction. Hence this Roth-like treatment would be compatible with the logic of a consumed-income tax.[6]

This logic assumes that the insurance payout is in the form of an annuity—a stream of annual or monthly payments to the survivor for some extended period of time. However, many life insurance policies pay just a lump sum amount. To allow the survivor to maintain this Roth-like treatment, the entire lump sum insurance payout should be Roth-IRA eligible. Since this payout is intended to provide a reasonably sure and predictable replacement income for the survivor, the limits on the types of assets that can be held in a Roth IRA are entirely appropriate.

This would in turn require raising the cap on Roth IRA assets. The cleanest treatment would be to allow the payout recipient to hold an "insurance" Roth, with an initial cap equal to the amount of the insurance payout that is deposited within one year. The recipient's other Roth IRAs would continue to have a combined $250,000 cap. Thereafter, the cap on the "insurance" Roth would be the previous month's ending balance, so funds could be withdrawn, but not added. All of the fund's investment earning would need to be withdrawn, which should naturally occur anyway, since the insurance fund is presumably providing replacement income for the survivor.

There are two obvious advantages of giving Roth-like treatment to these various kinds of income protection insurance. First, this is the simplest treatment. There is nothing to report for tax purposes when you buy the insurance, and there is nothing to report for tax purposes if you happen to receive a payout. Second, it's how we currently tax these forms of insurance. So I would recommend that we stay with the status quo.

However, this status quo leaves an opening for abuse. A millionaire could buy life insurance policies with his or her heirs listed as beneficiaries, leaving an inheritance that escapes the inheritance tax. This is not an issue when the beneficiary is a spouse, as is usually the case, since an estate that is left to a surviving spouse is not considered an inheritance. So I would add that this Roth-treatment of insurance, including the higher Roth cap, be limited to surviving spouses, with perhaps some provisions for surviving minor children. For others, the insurance proceeds should be treated like any other form of inheritance, fully taxable but fully IRA eligible.

It would be inappropriate however to give Roth-like treatment to employer-provided insurance, while also allowing the employer to deduct the premiums, unless those premiums are reported as part of the employee's income.

For income-liability insurance, which protects the incomes of others against a death or injury that you caused, again Roth-like treatment makes sense. Income-liability insurance is often combined with self-property and property-liability insurance in homeowner and auto insurance policies, so treating all of these forms of insurance identically simplifies our tax treatment of insurance. This would also add a small insurance-related tax-redistribution component to the tax code, but making the liable parties (who can't deduct their premiums) liable for the taxes paid on the payout to the injured parties (who would not owe taxes on their insurance proceeds).

HEALTH INSURANCE

The consumption of health care, whether paid for through health insurance or out of pocket, presents something of a problem under just about any tax system. The fundamental question we need to ask is, do we count it as consumption?

I think mostly the answer is no. If John spends $50,000 this year to pay for his lifestyle, and Joe spends $100,000 this year to pay for the exact same lifestyle plus chemotherapy, has Joe consumed "more" than John, in the sense of having a better standard of living? My guess is, we'd both agree that the answer is no. Joe's extra spending was just dealing with a problem that John was lucky enough not to have. There are certainly exceptions we can identify, like many types of elective surgery. But mostly, I don't think we want to consider most health care expenditures as "consumption."

Our current tax system supports the idea that we think of health care consumption as different from other types of consumption. Employer-provided health insurance is not counted as taxable income, which is effectively a significant health insurance subsidy. We have health savings accounts that allow tax deductions for contributions, but tax-free withdrawals when the withdrawal pays for medical care. And we allow a deduction for any medical costs that exceed 10% of Adjusted Gross Income.

If we've decided not to consider "qualified" medical expenses as consumption, our current tax treatment also makes sense under a consumed-income tax. Income spent buying health insurance would not be "consumed," and so it should be excluded from taxation. Similarly, income spent on medical care should be deductible. And any health care we receive that is covered by health insurance should not be taxed.

The adoption of the Affordable Care Act (aka Obamacare) introduced another series of health care subsidies into our tax code, for individuals who do not get employer-provided health insurance. These subsidies are quite different from those provided to people with employer-provided health insurance. The Obamacare subsidies are typically somewhat better for low-income families and significantly lower for high-income families. That may not make much economic sense, but it probably makes political sense, at least for now.

Ideally, our tax system should treat health care costs, and health insurance, more rationally that we currently do. In an ideal world, health insurance subsidies would not be tied to where one works, and the subsidies for those getting their health insurance directly from some market exchange would exactly match the subsidies for those getting their health insurance through their employment.

But this is not an ideal world. And with all the emotional baggage currently attached to this issue, it is probably best to conclude that our current tax treatment of health care and health insurance creates no major problems for a consumed-income tax, and we should leave well enough, or bad enough, alone.

A portion of liability insurance covers the health care costs of those we injure. It makes no sense to tax the injured parties on the health care they receive, so it should make no sense to allow the liability insurance premiums to be deducted. Admittedly, that is not consistent with how we treat the health insurance we buy to protect ourselves. But again, since this health-liability insurance is usually combined with other forms of insurance in a single policy, providing a deduction for one portion of the premiums, but not other portions, is just inviting abuse.

UNEMPLOYMENT INSURANCE

Unemployment insurance protects workers in cyclical industries from income losses due to layoffs. The premiums are collected from their employers and paid into a state and a federal fund, based in part on the business' layoff history. Those funds in turn pay unemployment compensation to any laid off workers. The employers are allowed to deduct the premiums as a cost of hiring workers, so logically, the workers should be taxed on any unemployment compensation they receive.

Since that is our current tax treatment of unemployment compensation, no change would be needed.

In summary, the tax code changes I recommend for insurance are:

1. Eliminate special tax treatments:
    - Tax employer-paid insurance premiums as consumed income.
2. Limit Roth IRAs to low risk investments:
    - Allow lump sum insurance payouts under some circumstances to be fully deposited into "insurance" Roth IRAs, with temporarily high Roth IRA caps.

NOTES

1. Recall the discussion of Roth IRAs in chapter 5.
2. Mieszkowski (1980).

3. This 10% minimum is effectively a very large insurance deductible. It discourages taking the tax deduction for trivial losses, including the loss not covered by your insurance policy because of your policy's deductible.

4. This is the tax treatment recommended in Bradford et al. (1984).

5. To be a bit more technically accurate, either way the employer gets the same deduction, as a cost of employing me. If part of my employment cost is the insurance he pays for, that's really income to me, but I get to exclude it for tax purposes. That is effectively identical to my getting a deduction.

6. However, Bradford et al. (1984) recommended that these forms of insurance be given the traditional IRA tax treatment: premiums deductible, payouts taxed.

Chapter Eleven

The Corporate Income Tax

Thus far, I have focused entirely on reforming the personal income tax. But what about the corporate income tax? Doesn't that need reformed as well? Absolutely.

Although the personal income tax is a mess, the corporate income tax is far worse. It distorts corporate behavior along a whole series of dimensions, and it is easily manipulated, resulting in a ton of tax avoidance. We will take a look at each of those problems, one at a time. But first, a comment on why we have corporations, and which corporations do and don't pay the corporate income tax.

In essence, a corporation is nothing more than a legal arrangement that provides its owners with limited liability. If you invest one-fourth of your life savings into a joint venture—let's suppose it's a restaurant that you, I, and three of our friends open—and it goes bankrupt, you could lose that one big chunk of your life savings, but not the other three-fourths. That is, your liability is limited just to the amount that you invested, and no more. This limited liability makes it safer for you to passively invest in enterprises that you don't control on a day-to-day basis, and makes business ventures with many owners much more feasible.

Although the corporate structure makes possible very large businesses with thousands of shareholder-investors, most corporations are rather small. In 2014 for example, almost 90% of all corporations employed fewer than 20 workers, and 98% had fewer than 100 workers.[1] Most of these small corporations choose to file as "S corporations" that are exempt from the corporate income tax. Instead, all of their profits are imputed to their owners, who then have to pay the personal income tax on those profits. So for example, if you and I were to form a corporation, each of us holding half the shares, and that corporation earns $10,000 in profits, we would each have to report $5,000 in income from that corporation when we file our income taxes, *whether we had the corporation actually pay those profits out to us or not*. Thus, S corporations are taxed the same way as small businesses, which in most cases, they are.

In contrast, if we own shares in a "C corporation"—the kind that does pay the corporate income tax—we would only have to declare any dividends paid to us, or any capital gains when we sold our shares. We would not have to pay personal income taxes on any profits retained by the corporation. But the corporation would have to pay corporate income taxes on all of its profits, whether paid out as dividends or retained.

Many C corporations are very large, with hundreds, thousands, or even hundreds of thousands of shareholders. The firms in the S&P500 are C corporations, as are most of the companies who own the brand names you'll immediately recognize—Apple, Coca-Cola, Delta, Fritos, GM, Kleenex, Sara Lee, and so on. Many C corporations are multinationals, with subsidiaries in countries all across the globe. Those are the ones we are primarily thinking about when we talk about the problems with the corporate income tax, both in terms of the distortions in behavior, and in terms of tax avoidance.

So why do some corporations grow so much larger than all the rest? There are three answers to that question: economies of scale, network economics, and intellectual property.

To understand economies of scale, imagine you are manufacturing automobiles in a large garage, one or two autos at a time. Producing a car involves a lot of steps: cutting sheets of metal and bending them into shape, welding components together, assembling the body, and so on. In your garage, each step would involve getting out the right tools, doing the task, and then putting everything away before starting the next step.

If, however, you were manufacturing not one or two cars at a time but fifty or one hundred in a vast factory, you could have hundreds of different work stations, each permanently set up for a particular task—in other words, an assembly line. Each car would have its metal sheets cut out over here, then bent into the appropriate shapes there and there and there, and so on. The final product would roll out of the factory only after passing through each of the many work stations. Because autos are being produced on a massive scale, all of the costs associated with setting stations up and then taking them down again are saved. As a result, a massive auto company can produce cars at a substantially lower cost than a small company can.

Most manufacturing involves some degree of economies of scale. But those economies of scale are more important in some industries than in others. Industries with larger economies of scale will be more dominated by larger businesses, and will have a smaller number of producers competing to sell you their product. That reduced competitive pressure makes it more likely that the individual businesses will be earning monopoly profits, that is, infra-marginal returns.

Economies of scale give large producers an advantage over small producers, because of production cost. Network economics, in contrast, give companies with large consumer bases an advantage over companies with small consumer bases, because of consumer demand. Suppose I start up a new online social network, called Look-At-This. You could sign up for it free, and post your latest news and photos on it for all your friends to see. But all your friends are already using Facebook. So why would you choose my social network instead of the one that is already popular?

Network economics implies that once a particular social network arises, only one company will survive (remember MySpace?). That is, there can be only one Facebook and only one Twitter and so on. Once a company has filled a particular network niche, it will have no direct competitors—and again, will potentially be able to earn monopoly profits/infra-marginal returns.

Intellectual property, the third source of potential monopolies, includes patents, copyrights, and trademarks. If a pharmaceutical company discovers a new medication and receives a patent for its discovery, it will be the only business allowed to manufacture and sell that medication for the next 20 years. If someone creates a new software application and copyrights their creation, they and their heirs will have the exclusive right to sell that software until 70 years after the creator dies. And if a company creates and registers a trademark that consumers identify with—say, a set of golden arches on all its fast food establishments—it can sell franchise rights to use that trademark for as long as it maintains that trademark.

Relatively few patents, copyrights, or trademarks result in businesses that are enormously profitable. But almost all of the really large corporations that are enormously profitable can attribute much of that profit to the intellectual property that they own. And it is hard to explain why multinational corporations would even exist without invoking at least one and often several forms of intellectual property.

So in short, some corporations become massive as a way to fully exploit their economies of scale, network economics, and/or intellectual property. And those economies of scale, network economics, and/or intellectual property in turn often result in infra-marginal returns.

Having a corporate income tax allows us to double-tax those infra-marginal returns, but at a cost. As I noted above, the corporate income tax we currently have distorts corporate behavior along a whole series of dimensions, and is easily manipulated, resulting in a ton of tax avoidance. Is it possible to devise a corporate income tax that is less distorting and less avoidable?

CORPORATE BEHAVIOR DISTORTIONS

In a sense, the current corporate income tax looks just like our current tax on other businesses. Corporations add up all of their sales revenue, subtract out costs (like wages paid and materials purchased), subtract their depreciation allowances and interest paid, and then pay a tax on the balance. In theory, multinational corporations owe taxes even on their profits earned outside the U.S. In practice however, profits earned abroad before 2018 were only taxed when they were "repatriated," that is, when the foreign subsidiary paid those profits back to the U.S. parent corporation as a dividend. And as we've seen already, a tax that can be delayed is a tax with a lower rate.[2]

As a result, U.S. corporations are taxed at different effective rates, depending on where they earn their profits. This gives them an incentive to invest in low-tax countries rather than high-tax countries, distorting those investment decisions.[3] Because they can deduct their interest payments, corporations have an incentive to finance those investments more through debt than through shareholder equity, distorting their financing decisions.[4] U.S. corporations are taxed on their worldwide profits, but foreign corporations like VW are only taxed on the profits they earn in the U.S. That gives a U.S. corporation an incentive to "invert." That is, the U.S. corporation merges with a foreign corporation, declares the foreign corporation as the parent corporation, and names the U.S. corporation as the foreign subsidiary, even though in many cases the "subsidiary" is many times larger than the "parent."[5]

Corporations can also avoid taxation by relocating their profits to other, lower-tax countries. Strategies like "transfer pricing" allow many U.S. corporations to report almost no U.S. profits, and thus pay little to no U.S. corporate income taxes, despite being very profitable worldwide. One form of transfer pricing involves a subsidiary in a low-tax country, which sells some component to its parent company at an inflated price. Another involves relocating intellectual property, with the corporation selling a patent to its low-tax foreign subsidiary at a low price, and then paying that subsidiary a high fee for the right to use that patent.[6]

So what should we do with this mess? We should reform the corporate income tax, not eliminate it. Eliminating it would provide a windfall gain to shareholders. If someone bought shares in the XYZ Corporation last month, they did so with some expectation about both XYZ's future profitability, and the future tax treatment of those expected profits. If we suddenly eliminated the corporate income tax, and wiped out all of those future tax liabilities, that would increase the value of XYZ's shares.[7]

This windfall gain to the holders of this old wealth would come at the expense of current and future taxpayers. Eliminating the corporate income tax on old wealth would reduce tax revenues, without creating any offsetting positive incentive effects. This revenue loss would have to be made up with higher tax rates on other consumed income, and as a result, greater disincentives to working.[8]

Preventing such windfall gains is especially important, since many U.S. corporations have many foreign shareholders.[9] Under our current tax system, their share of corporate earnings is taxed, so they indirectly pay taxes to the U.S. government. But that is only appropriate. Their corporation uses the U.S. transportation network. Their corporation uses the U.S. legal system. Their investments are protected by the U.S. military. So why would we want to wipe out all of their future tax liabilities?

The corporate income tax should also not be eliminated because it, like a traditional IRA, will tax any infra-marginal returns (or "excess profits") on investment.[10] As we saw above, large corporations are particularly likely to have high yielding intangible assets, including such intellectual properties as patents, trademarks, and brand-name recognition.[11] As we saw in chapter 5, a tax on infra-marginal returns generates tax revenue without having any effect on the incentives to save or invest. Indeed, if we could figure out exactly how to do it, the ideal tax system would tax only infra-marginal returns at a very high rate, and nothing else.

But although it makes sense to continue to have a corporate income tax, it makes no sense to continue to have our current corporate income tax. Is it possible to generate that significant amount of tax revenue, without all of those distortions? The answer is yes—by adopting three major reforms. The first reform would involve making the exact same changes proposed for small businesses—expensing new investment, and taxing new debt. That would eliminate the distortions in most investment decisions and the distortions in financing decisions. As with small business, corporations could be allowed to issue nontaxable debt, with no deduction for interest payments. Or they could be allowed to issue taxable debt, where the amounts borrowed are taxable and the interest and principle payments are deductible. Either debt tax treatment would remove the tax advantage of debt financing over equity financing for corporations.[12] As with small businesses, I recommend sticking strictly to the nontaxable debt treatment.

Adding these provisions to the corporate income tax would effectively convert it to a "cash flow tax," which as we've seen is a tax only on infra-marginal returns, or what in this context economists term a tax on "economic rents."[13] These provisions would also eliminate the corporate tax code's bias toward debt-financed investment over equity-financed investment. Using the tax code to encourage excessive corporate leveraging, which leads to greater bankruptcy risk during recessions, makes no sense whatsoever. But that is exactly what our current tax system does.

The second major reform would solve the corporate inversion problem: switch from a worldwide corporate tax system to a destination-based corporate tax system. We do not tax the German company Volkswagen AG when it produces and sells cars in Europe and Asia, but only when its American subsidiary Volkswagen Group of America Inc. sells cars in the U.S. So why would we tax Ford's European subsidiary Ford of Europe AG when it produces and sells cars in Europe? Since we currently only tax Ford of Europe's profits if it pays them as dividends to its U.S. parent company Ford Inc., we collect a relatively small amount of revenue from worldwide taxation. It would make far more sense to just tax the profits corporations earn in the U.S.—both those of VW of America and Ford Inc.—at (if necessary) a slightly higher tax rate, and eliminate the incentive to invert.

Switching to a destination-based corporate income tax would increase somewhat the incentive to relocate profits to low-tax countries. So switching to a destination-based system, needs to be accompanied with a solution to the profit-shifting problem.

CORPORATE TAX AVOIDANCE

Before describing the third major reform, let me discuss in greater detail the profit-shifting problem our current corporate income tax has. Mostly, this problem is the result of a so-called transfer prices.

Suppose you have a 2010 Chevy that you want to sell. Before posting an ad for it in your local newspaper or on some online website, you'll need to determine a reasonable asking price. To do that, you'll probably find some resource like Kelly's Blue Book, that tells you what a typical 2010 Chevy sells for. You adjust that number up or down a little, depending on what condition your car is in and how eager you are to get it sold, and there's your price.

You do that because you want to get a fair price for your car. You also expect the buyer will be willing to pay no more than a fair price, whoever that buyer may turn out to be. And that's the issue—you don't know who they'll be. They're probably going to be a stranger to you, someone you otherwise don't particularly know or care about. And so the sale of the car to them will be the sale to a stranger, or what economists call an "arm's-length" transaction.

Suppose, however, that just before posting the ad for your car, you hear that one of your nieces or nephews is looking to buy a used car to take to college. You're now less concerned about getting that same fair price for the car. Since you're thinking about selling to a family member, the notion of what might be the "fair" price is entirely different. Maybe you've done pretty well in life, and can afford to give that niece or nephew a little bit of a price break. Perhaps, after talking it over with your spouse, it only seems right to offer to sell the car at a price substantially below the Blue Book value—because you're no longer selling to a stranger, no longer making an arm's-length transaction.

Now let's take it one step further. You own a small business, a pizza company that owns a car that was used to deliver pizzas. The business no longer needs this car, but you do, to give to one of your own kids who's going off to college. So you decide to have the business "sell" you the car. What price do you charge yourself? It could be the Blue Book price, but then again, it could be any other price you want it to be. Because really, you're just selling it to yourself, and all the money you pay out of your right-hand pocket is just going to end up in your left-hand pocket anyway. So the price you charge is totally arbitrary. Economists call this price a "transfer price."

Corporations use transfer prices to move profits from one country to another. Suppose Ford Motor Co. is selling 100 cars, all manufactured in the U.S., to its German subsidiary. Suppose the "fair" price is $20,000 a car. If Ford sold these cars for say $25,000, its U.S. corporate division would make an extra $500,000 in profit, and its German subsidiary would make $500,000 less in profit. If instead Ford transferred the cars for $15,000 each, U.S. profits would drop $500,000 and Germany profits would rise that much. By manipulating the transfer price, Ford can either shift profits from Germany into the U.S., or from the U.S. into Germany, whichever would be more advantageous. If its profits in Germany are taxed at a different effective rate than its profits in the U.S., one of those shifts will be advantageous.

Of course, the IRS knows about this strategy, and does its best to block it, which is why Ford's transfer price manipulation would not work. The IRS can observe the price Ford sells its cars to its U.S. dealerships. Since these dealers are generally separate companies, not owned by Ford, these are arm's-length transactions. Then the IRS can, and does, insist that the sale of these same cars to the German subsidiary be priced at the same price. When arm's-length transactions are easily observable, transfer price manipulation is easy to prevent.

But suppose Ford-U.S. is charging Ford-Germany a licensing fee for the use of the Ford logo. If that licensing fee is high, Ford will have higher U.S. profits and lower Germany profits; if that licensing fee is low, Ford will have lower U.S. profits, and higher Germany profits. Even if Ford licenses its logo to other entities—say, its Brazilian subsidiary, or all those dealerships with a Ford logo on their signage—it's hard to say what the "correct" license fees should be. That gives Ford a lot more leeway in moving its profits from one country to another, and the IRS relatively little ability to prevent that manipulation from happening.

Large U.S. corporations move a ton of profits from the U.S. to a variety of tax havens, using the transfer pricing of hard-to-price intellectual property rights. Is it mere coincidence that Apple, Microsoft, and Google have all moved many of their patents and copyrights to low-tax Ireland, and have their Irish subsidiaries charge their U.S. operations enormous fees to use those patents and copyrights? Or are they all using the same tax-avoidance strategy? I'm pretty sure it's the latter.[14]

So what's the solution to this problem?

ELIMINATING CORPORATE TAX SHIFTING

The third reform would eliminate this profit-shifting problem. Two alternative solutions have been put forward, both involving a shift to destination-based taxation: border adjustment and formula apportionment. My recommendation is to go the formula apportionment route. But before discussing that option, let's look at the border adjustment proposal.

Border adjustment is usually discussed as a part of an X-tax, where all non-labor income is taxed at the business level and there's no distinction between corporations and other businesses. Using it with a consumed-income tax may be somewhat awkward. Under border adjustment, all items imported into the U.S. would be taxed at the business/corporate tax rate, and all items exported from the U.S. would get a tax rebate equal to the business/corporate tax rate. Thus, under border adjustment, any item destined to be sold in the U.S., whether produced here or abroad, would be taxed, and any item destined to be sold abroad, again whether produced here or abroad, would go untaxed. Voila, a destination-based business tax.

As you may recall from the table manufacturer example in chapter 4, this is how imports and exports work under a value added tax (VAT). However, under a VAT the producers are taxed on the full sales price of their product, minus any (already taxed) goods used to produce that product—the table manufacturer being taxed on the $50 table minus the $20 lumber. In contrast, under an X-tax or consumed-income tax, the manufacturer would also be allowed to deduct the wages they pay. And that difference creates issues.

Suppose we now have two table manufacturers, one in the U.S. and the other in Canada, producing identical $50 tables. The U.S. company buys $20 of U.S. lumber and pays its workers $20 per table, so it is taxed on its $10 profit if it sells the table in the U.S. The Canadian company, in contrast, is taxed on the entire $50 sale price under border adjustment if it sells a table in the U.S. And the U.S. company, if it sells its $50 table in Canada, gets a $50 tax deduction—so each table it exports to Canada allows it to cancel out the taxes on five tables sold in the U.S.

It is almost certain that border adjustment, if adopted, would be in violation of World Trade Organization (WTO) rules. Article III, paragraph 2 of the 1994 General Agreement on Tariffs and Trade (GATT) states that "The products of the territory of any contracting party imported into the territory of any other contracting party shall not be subject, directly or indirectly, to internal taxes or other internal charges of any kind in excess of those applied, directly or indirectly, to like domestic products." Taxing a Canadian table or any other foreign-made table at a five times higher rate than the tax on an American table would certainly be seen by those countries as violating Article III. It would be met at minimum by an appeal to the WTO to declare the border-adjustment tax in violation of the rules. At maximum, there would be an all-out trade war.

But suppose the WTO were somehow convinced not to rule against the U.S. tax. Proponents of border adjustment argue that any trade imbalance would disappear through exchange rate adjustments. Suppose that before the border adjustment tax, the U.S. dollar and Canadian dollars traded one-for-one. Suppose also that the corporate/business tax rate were 40%, so the Canadian table that had previous sold for C$50 would under border adjustment sell for C$70. If the exchange rate between the U.S. dollar and the Canadian dollar adjusted upward to where one U.S. dollar (US$1) traded for 1.4 Canadian dollars (C$1.40), then it would take only US$50 to buy the C$70 table. So both the U.S. and the Canadian tables would again sell for $50 here in the U.S. Therefore border adjustment, its proponents argue, would give U.S. firms no unfair tax advantage whatsoever.[15]

While this argument is quite reasonable, it ignores the fact that the exchange rate adjustment would be less than instantaneous.[16] Initially, the American tables would sell for 40% less than the Canadian tables, both here in the U.S. and in Canada. Sales of U.S. tables would rise, and sales of Canadian tables would totally disappear. The U.S. would run a huge trade surplus, and foreigners would be eager to trade their currencies for U.S. dollars to buy the suddenly-40%-cheaper U.S. products. That rush to buy dollars would gradually drive up the value of the dollar, until eventually it would be 40% stronger, and we would be back to equilibrium.

But in the meantime, a lot of small businesses in Canada would have gone out of business. It might take decades before new Canadian businesses are reborn, and can re-establish their positions in markets that had been taken over by their American competitors. So no, I don't think the Canadian government, or the governments of any of our other trading partners, would be likely to stand by idly and wait for the magic new equilibrium to establish itself. And besides, even if all of this occurred without a trade war being unleashed, what would happen to the U.S. tourism industry and U.S. higher education, now that the cost of visiting the U.S. or attending its universities is 40% higher for foreigners?

In addition, it is important to keep in mind that much of the world's trade is carried out in dollars. If a Brazilian company wants to write a long-term sales contract with a Liberian company, the prices in that contract are typically set in dollars. A 40% rise in the dollar would wreck havoc in international markets and could well set off a worldwide economic downturn.

All in all, I find border adjustment a fascinating theoretical solution that totally falls apart once it hits reality. And that is exactly what happened when it was introduced into the Republican tax plan in early 2017. The political backlash sunk the proposal almost immediately. I'm interested in identifying tax reform options that have at least a prayer of being adopted. So I would strongly recommend against any proposal involving border adjustment.

That leaves formula apportionment, a tax strategy that our state governments have been using for nearly a century.[17] Notice that this exact same profit-shifting problem bedevils state tax collectors. Ford-Michigan buys steel from the steel plant in Gary owned by Ford-Indiana, engine parts from Ford-Ohio, and so on. It could use transfer prices to freely move profits from one state to another, until most if not all of those profits are located in the lowest-taxing state. So to prevent this, the states divide Ford's total U.S. profits among themselves, using formulas based on where Ford's capital assets (factories, equipment, etc.) are located, where its workforce is located, and where its sales are located.

For example, suppose Ford has $100 million in U.S. profits, and Kentucky uses a formula that puts 1/3rd weight on each of those three factors.[18] Suppose also that Ford has 7% of its plant and equipment, 8% of its workforce, and 3% of its sales located in Kentucky. Then by the apportionment formula, Ford would have to pay taxes on $(7\% + 8\% + 3\%)/3 = 6\%$ of its profits, $6 million, in Kentucky.

Because state taxes are based on total Ford-U.S. profits, Ford cannot change its tax liabilities by adjusting some transfer price between Ford-Michigan and Ford-Ohio.[19] However, it can change its tax liabilities by moving a factory to a state whose formula does not involve business assets or labor force. For that reason, states have increasingly moved toward a formula based entirely on sales. Under that pure sales-apportionment, Kentucky would tax Ford solely on the 3% of sales located in Kentucky, so Ford would pay taxes on just $3 million in Kentucky. The downside, for a state like Kentucky that has corporate manufacturing operations within its borders, is that it would collect less in tax revenues. The upside is that those manufacturers would no longer have any incentive to move their operations elsewhere.

So what should our federal government do? Adopting a corporate cash-flow tax would mean it would only be taxing pure profits. These are generated by charging consumers higher prices in markets where the corporation has some degree of monopoly power, typically due to its patents, trademarks, and brand-name recognition. Logically, those profits should be taxed where they are generated, which is where the corporation's products are sold. So the logical choice would be for the U.S. to adopt single-factor sales apportionment on worldwide profits for all of the corporations that do business in the U.S.[20]

The beauty of this combination of reforms—sales apportionment and cash-flow taxation—is that the corporate income tax would no longer distort any production or financing decisions whatsoever. Locate your factory in Michigan, Mexico, or Mozambique, you are taxed the same. Move the headquarters of your company to Pittsburgh, Portugal, or Peru, and the exact same 23% of your worldwide economic profits are taxed, based solely of the 23% of sales located here in the U.S. All of those decisions would then be based solely on what makes economic sense, not on what the tax code (often unintentionally) discourages.[21]

This is not to say that there would be no attempts to avoid taxation. Sales apportionment creates a small incentive for a multinational business with above-normal profits to sell its products in high tax countries at a slightly higher price than it would sell in low tax countries.[22] This is unavoidable in a world where different jurisdictions are able to set their own tax rates, and suggests that extremely high tax rates should be avoided.

Corporations would also have an incentive to spread profits to low tax areas by acquiring low profit divisions. If Apple Computer starts selling apples—the fruit, not the computer—in South America, under sales apportionment, it might have a large share of all its profits taxed at low South American tax rates. To prevent this, profits should be apportioned separately for separate industries; computer profits apportioned by computer sales, fruit profits apportioned by fruit sales. The boundaries between industries are easier to observe and enforce than the boundaries between countries—the fruit-apples sold to the computer-Apple division to sell in its cafeterias and the computer-Apples used by the fruit-apple division to keep track of its orchard production both have easy-to-observe arm's-length prices, that allow the profits of each division to be easily segregated. Therefore, although tax avoidance games will undoubtedly still be played, they will be played on a playing field that is nowhere as heavily tilted in the corporations' favor.

Similarly, corporations would have an incentive to relocate their sales to low-tax jurisdictions. If Apple sold all of its U.S.-bound iPhones to the Bermuda divisions of Walmart, Best Buy, Verizon, and other iPhone retailers, it could claim that all of its profits were earned not in the U.S. but in Bermuda. To prevent this, the location of sales would have to be legally defined as the location of final sale, so that Apple would have to keep track of, and report to the government, exactly what fraction of all of its iPhones ended up in the U.S. Of course, Apple already knows the location of all of its iPhones, but I'm sure many of these extremely profitable corporations will complain about the burden of keeping track of all of those final sale locations. Remember though, they started this move-the-profits-away game, so if it creates a record keeping burden for them, they brought it on themselves.

This record keeping should be limited to where the intellectual property is visible. Monsanto is a multinational agri-business that sells seeds, fertilizers, weed killers, and a variety of other products for farmers around the world. Its products are used to produce corn, soybeans, and many other crops. Keeping track of where all these crops end up would be an impossible task, and an unnecessary one. When you buy cotton underwear, you have no idea whether the cotton was grown using any of Monsanto's products. The Monsanto trademark is not visible to you. So Monsanto should only be required to report what fraction of its Dekalb® seeds and Roundup® herbicide are ultimately sold in the U.S. However, if Intel's computer chips are an integral part of Dell's computers—that is, if the trademark Dell implies to consumers that the computer has "Intel inside"—then Intel will need to keep track, through Dell and the other companies it supplies, where its computer chips ultimately end up.[23]

Of course, those changes, plus any other loophole-closing reforms that might be adopted, would require some appropriate adjustment of the corporate income tax rate. Since these changes would allow firms to immediately write off new investment, and would no longer tax profits generated in other countries, tax revenues would tend to fall. But since these changes would also eliminate interest deductions, and would once again tax profits generated in the U.S. that are currently hidden in other countries through transfer pricing and other similar schemes, tax revenues would tend to rise. And since the combined changes would convert the corporate income tax into a tax on only old wealth and any economic rents on new wealth, the tax rate could in fact be increased somewhat with hardly any undesirable consequences.

In summary, the corporate tax code changes I recommend are:

1. Expense new capital investment:
   - Allow new capital equipment to be immediately and fully expensed (or depreciated over its lifetime, with the undepreciated value carried forward at the risk-free interest rate).

2. Give new corporate debt nontaxable treatment:
   * Eliminate the interest deduction for new corporate debt.
3. Adopt worldwide sales apportionment:
   * Tax a share of corporate worldwide profits, based on the share of its sales located in the U.S.

NOTES

1. U.S. Small Business Administration (2018).

2. Grubert (1998), Altschuler and Grubert (2002).

3. Desai et al. (2004), Becker and Riedel (2012).

4. Mills and Newberry (2004), Huizinga et al. (2008), Arena and Roper (2010). Kleinbard (2007) provides a nice description of why the tax code's debt/equity distinction makes little economic sense.

5. The 2018 Tax Cuts and Jobs Act, which Donald Trump signed into law in December 2017, reduced but did not eliminate our taxation of U.S. corporations' worldwide profits. We'll discuss these changes in chapter 13.

6. Bartelsman and Beetsma (2003), Clausing (2003); Dischinger and Riedel (2011), Karkinski and Riedel (2012), Griffith et al. (2014). Keightley (2013) found that "American companies reported earning 43% of [their] overseas profits in Bermuda, Ireland, Luxembourg, the Netherlands, and Switzerland in 2008, while hiring 4% of their foreign workforce and making 7% of their foreign investments in those economies"—a clear indication of tax-avoiding profit shifting—and that this profit-shifting has been increasing over time.

7. Aaron and Galper (1985), Bradford (1986), King (1987).

8. Alternatively, if we really want to decrease the government's tax revenue, we should reduce the tax rate on consumed income, and reduce any disincentive effects it creates on work behavior, rather than eliminate the corporate income tax on old wealth, which would not create any similar disincentive reductions.

9. Aaron and Galper (1985), King (1987).

10. Bradford (1986), Aaron and Galper (1985).

11. A considerable share of the current corporate income tax base—around 63%, according to Cronin et al. (2013)—can be attributed to supernormal returns.

12. Kleinbard (2007) discusses the issues involved in levying a tax on the normal returns earned by business enterprises, which would make sense under a traditional income tax but not under a consumed-income tax. The complexity of his proposal for levying such a tax is a strong argument for consumed-income taxation.

13. Studies advocating cash flow taxation include OECD (2007), Auerbach, Devereux and Simpson (2010), and Institute for Fiscal Studies (2011).

14. Zucman (2014) provides a very nice description of how this is done, and shows that this is a rapidly growing problem.

15. Bond and Devereux (2002), Auerbach and Devereux (2015).

16. I was recently asked, after expressing my skepticism about border adjustment, whether I "believed in market equilibrium." Yes, I believe in market equilibrium; that

is, I believe that disequilibrium unleashes dynamic forces that cause prices to adjust until a new equilibrium is established. But no, I don't believe that this happens after some instantaneous waving of the hands.

17. Formula apportionment has been recommended by the European Commission (2001) for the E.U., and advocated by Avi-Yonah et al. (2009) for the U.S. and Eichner and Runkel (2008) for the E.U.

18. Historically, most states used this three-factor "Massachusetts" formula that gave equal weight to all three factors. Since 1990, most states have gravitated to a formula that weighs sales more heavily than either business assets or labor payroll.

19. However, Ford could reduce its state taxes by moving profits from Ford-U.S. to Ford-elsewhere. For this reason, a few states, most notably California, have begun using formulas based on worldwide profits.

20. Hines (2010) provides empirical evidence for the optimality of sales-based formula apportionment. He estimated how corporate profits are related to sales, plant and equipment (i.e., capital), and labor force employment (measured by total labor compensation). He found no relationship between profits and labor compensation—so no weight should be given to employment share when profits are apportioned. He also found that sales had over twice the impact on profits as property, plant, and equipment.

To put that latter result into perspective, Cronin et al. (2013) found that 63% of the U.S. corporate income tax falls on super-normal profits, and 36% falls on the normal return to capital and labor. Combining that with Hines's results suggests that the optimal apportionment formula assigns any tax on the normal return to capital in proportion to the distribution of property, plant, and equipment, and any tax on super-normal profits in proportion to sales Thus, for a cash-flow corporate tax, i.e., a tax only on pure profits, the Hines-Cronin results suggest sales apportionment is pretty much exactly correct.

21. Essentially all that are being apportioned are costs. If a company generates 23% of its sales revenue in the U.S., all of that revenue would be subject to U.S. taxation. It would then be able to deduct from that revenue 23% of its worldwide labor, supplies, and depreciation/expensing costs, regardless of where those costs were incurred.

22. McGee (2017).

23. There should be a "100% U.S." option available for corporations concerned about the cost of this record keeping. They would report all of their revenues as being earned in the U.S., be allowed to deduct all of their costs in the U.S., and have all of their profits taxed under the U.S. corporate income tax. For most small U.S. corporations, this would both eliminate having to mess with this type of record keeping and be an exactly accurate description of their situation. However, this option should also be available to any corporation that might find it preferable.

Chapter Twelve

Tax Expenditures

The Congressional Budget Act of 1974 defined "tax expenditures" as "revenue losses . . . which allow a special exclusion, exemption, or deduction from gross income or which provide a special credit, a preferential rate of tax, or a deferral of tax liability." In other words, tax expenditures are special tax breaks that allow some individuals to pay less in taxes than everyone else.[1]

There are in general three reasons why we have tax expenditures in our tax system. One of them is a good reason: we want to encourage good behaviors, like getting a higher education, and the tax code is a convenient place to create that encouragement. The second reason is a bad reason: special interest groups are sometimes able to get special tax treatments inserted into the tax code that benefit them and them alone. (Of course, what I consider good public policy you might consider an inappropriate sop to some special interest group, and vice versa.)

The third reason for tax expenditures is definitional: some provisions are considered tax expenditures only because they don't conform with the ideal of a traditional income tax. Moving to a consumed-income tax would eliminate many of these "definitional" tax expenditures, like IRAs, that make no sense under a traditional income tax but fit perfectly with a consumed-income tax.

As of October 2017, the Treasury Department's Office of Tax Analysis (OTA) identified 168 tax expenditures within our tax system. If we add up the revenue costs of these tax expenditures, they average a total of about $1.9 trillion a year in lost revenues over each of the next ten years. This number should be taken with a grain of salt: the OTA specifically warns against adding up tax expenditures. Due to the complexity of both economic behavior and our tax system, eliminating any one tax expenditure will change the costs associated with many of the remaining tax expenditures.

Nevertheless, this number can be taken as a rough estimate: there are a total of somewhere between $1.7 and $2.1 trillion in special tax treatments embedded in our tax code.

As noted above, some of these tax expenditures would no longer be "special" treatments, and would disappear if we switched to a consumed-income tax. Some would need to be eliminated, since they are entirely inconsistent with a consumed-income tax. And some could be either kept or eliminated, depending on how we choose to view them. Overall, if we adopted the reforms that I am recommending, the total number and volume of tax expenditures would decrease substantially.

TAX EXPENDITURES THAT WOULD BE NORMALIZED

As I noted above, tax expenditures are provisions that deviate from the "normal tax baseline," which is mostly based on the traditional income tax ideal.[2] Adopting the reforms recommended thus far in this book would change the baseline to that of a consumed-income tax, so a number of current tax expenditures would be "normalized," since they would not deviate from the new baseline.

Seven of the OTA's tax expenditures involve the special tax treatment of saving, for retirement, higher education, or medical spending. They are:

- Education Savings Accounts (ESAs);
- Medical Savings Accounts and Health Savings Accounts;
- Defined benefit employer plans;
- Defined contribution employer plans (e.g., 401(k)s);
- Individual Retirement Accounts (IRAs);
- Self-employed retirement plans; and
- Special Employee Stock Ownership Plan (ESOP) rules.

Under a consumed-income tax, these "special" tax treatments of saving would be extended to all forms of saving, so these would no longer be considered tax expenditures. Similarly, eight tax expenditures involve special provisions that allow certain industries to expense new investment. They are:

- Expensing of research and experimentation expenditures;
- Expensing of exploration and development costs, fuels;
- Expensing of exploration and development costs, nonfuel minerals;
- Expensing of multi-period timber growing costs;
- Expensing of certain agricultural capital outlays;

- Expensing of certain agricultural multiperiod production costs;
- Expensing of reforestation expenditures; and
- Expensing of certain small business investments.

Under a consumed-income tax, all industries would be able to expense new investment, so this tax treatment would no longer be "special."

Six other tax expenditures similarly provide tax treatment that makes sense under a consumed-income tax, but not under a traditional tax. They are:

- Exclusion of life insurance death benefits;
- Deductibility of casualty losses;
- Exclusion of interest spread of financial institutions;
- Exclusion of net imputed rental income;
- Qualified tuition programs; and
- Exclusion of employer-provided educational assistance.

As we saw in chapter 10, excluding life insurance death benefits would be perfectly appropriate under a consumed-income tax, provided the life insurance premiums were not deductible. We also saw that a casualty loss represents the loss of the consumption stream from a consumer durable. Under a consumed-income tax, the tax on that consumption stream is prepaid when the consumer durable is purchased. So a deduction for that loss, when it is sufficiently large, makes perfect sense under a consumed-income tax.

The "exclusion of interest spread" means you are not taxed on the banking services (like no-fee checking) that you get in lieu of interest on your checking and saving accounts. Under the reforms outlined in this book, these accounts would be treated as "tax prepaid" Roth IRAs, so any withdrawals—whether as principle, interest, or financial service—would be tax-free. Hence this current tax provision would make perfect sense under a consumed-income tax.

The "exclusion of net imputed rental income" refers to the "imputed rent" on owner-occupied housing mentioned in chapters 2 and 5. As we saw, not taxing imputed rent is a significant problem under a traditional income tax. But it makes perfect sense under a consumed-income tax, provided we eliminate the mortgage interest deduction.

"Qualified tuition programs" are the tax-exempt prepaid college tuition plans offered by many states. Under a consumed-income tax, these plans would qualify for Roth IRA treatment: no deduction when families deposit into these plans, and no tax when the funds are withdrawn. Hence these accounts would be fully normalized if we switch to a consumed-income tax.

Finally, the "exclusion of employer-provided educational assistance" lets employees earn tax-free "income" in the form of educational assistance. This violates the traditional income tax goal of taxing all income when it is earned. But purchasing education is an investment, which under a consumed-income tax should be expensed. As we will discuss below, this treatment of education spending will not generally make sense, since it conflicts with other social goals. But it works fine in the case of employer-provided assistance.[3]

Together, these 21 tax expenditures represent on average about $460 billion in revenue costs per year, or around one fourth of the total revenue cost of all tax expenditures. This demonstrates how much our current tax system, while nominally a traditional income tax, is loaded with provisions that only make sense under a consumed-income tax. It also suggests that moving the rest of the way to a consumed-income tax is the most reasonable way to achieve a sensible, cohesive, coherent tax system.

TAX EXPENDITURES THAT WOULD BECOME SUPERFLUOUS

Again, tax expenditures provide some individuals or some forms of income special treatment that other individuals or forms of income don't receive. Adopting the reforms recommended thus far in this book would provide to everyone the same treatment that several tax expenditures currently only provide to a few. Hence, those special treatments would become superfluous, since the treatment would no longer be special. The tax code provisions that allow these special treatments could then be eliminated.

Seven tax expenditures involve the accelerated depreciation of new investment. They are:

- Temporary 50 percent expensing for equipment used in the refining of liquid fuels (only applies to investments before 2014);
- Natural gas distribution pipelines treated as 15-year property;
- Amortize all geological and geophysical expenditures over two years;
- Allowance of deduction for certain energy efficient commercial building property;
- Accelerated depreciation on rental housing;
- Depreciation of buildings other than rental housing;
- Accelerated depreciation of machinery and equipment.

Under a consumed-income tax, all new investment would be expensed. Thus, all these tax treatments would be superseded by the new rules. An additional two tax expenditures provide tax breaks to holders of U.S. savings bonds. They are:

- Exclusion of interest on savings bonds redeemed to finance educational expenses, and
- Deferral of interest on U.S. savings bonds.

Under a consumed-income tax, savings bonds could be held either in traditional IRAs or Roth IRAs. Either way, effectively the interest would not be taxed, regardless of whether they were used to finance educational or other expenses.

There are four tax expenditures related to capital gains income:

- Deferral of capital gains from like-kind exchanges
- Deferral of gain on sales of farm refiners
- Step-up basis of capital gains at death, and
- Carryover basis of capital gains on gifts

The first two allow the sellers of specific assets to roll over their capital gains. Under my recommended reforms, this "special" tax treatment would be available to all investors.[4] Under the second two (a) heirs who inherit appreciated assets can sell and consume that wealth immediately, owing no taxes whatsoever, and (b) heirs who receive those assets as gifts can delay any taxes on the appreciated value until they sell those assets. Both provisions violate the traditional income tax ideal of taxing gains when they occur. Under the reforms recommended thus far in this book, these provisions would become superfluous. As outlined in chapter 9, inheritances and any gifts over $14,000 would be taxable income, fully eligible for IRA deposit, so the capital gains basis of those inherited assets would be irrelevant.

One tax expenditure allows farmers, but only farmers, to average their income for tax purposes:

- Income averaging for farmers.

Under a traditional income tax, this provision makes sense not just for farmers, but for any occupation where income varies radically from one year to the next. Under a consumed-income tax however, it is entirely unnecessary. If a farmer, or merchant, or actor, or anyone else has a particularly good year, they will be taxed that year only on the income they consume, not on the income they save. During a bad year, those savings can be withdrawn, consumed, and taxed. That is, since a consumed-income tax only taxes income when it is consumed, it allows individuals to even out their tax liabilities naturally, by evening out their spending. Thus, this "special" tax treatment would be available to everyone.

The last three tax expenditures relate to the corporate income tax:

- Inventory property sales source rules exception;
- Deferral of income from controlled foreign corporations;
- Deferred taxes for financial firms on certain income earned overseas.

Specifically, they refer to exceptions to the worldwide system that we had in place in 2017. All three would become superfluous if we adopt the corporate tax reforms recommended in chapter 11.

TAX EXPENDITURES FOR INDIVIDUALS THAT MUST BE ELIMINATED

There are a number of tax expenditures directed toward individuals that are entirely inconsistent with either a traditional income tax or a consumed-income tax. The first, and by far the largest, we've discussed already—the mortgage interest deduction:

- Mortgage interest expense on owner-occupied residences.

As we saw in chapter 6, this is an extremely poorly designed method to encourage home ownership, which should be replaced with something far less costly and far more effective.

Many of the other tax expenditures that absolutely need to go provide special treatment to one form of income over other forms of income. But under the logic of either a traditional income tax or a consumed-income tax, income is income is income, and all forms of income should be taxed the same, whether we tax that income when it is earned (traditional income tax) or when it is consumed (consumed-income tax).

Under our current income tax system, capital gains are taxed at one rate, "qualified" dividends at another. There are six tax expenditures related to these special tax rates:

- Capital gains treatment of royalties on coal;
- Capital gains treatment of certain timber;
- Capital gains treatment of certain agricultural income;
- Capital gains (except agriculture, timber, iron ore, and coal);
- Capital gains exclusion of small corporation stock; and
- Treatment of qualified dividends.

These special tax treatments add complexity to the tax code. In many cases they allow high-income taxpayers to pay lower tax rates than low-income taxpayers. Perhaps even worse, these special tax treatments encourage individuals to rearrange their investment or business decisions to get these special tax treatments. They also open up potential tax shelters, allowing high-income taxpayers to artificially convert other forms of income into favorably treated income.

These lower tax rates on dividends and capital gains are sometimes claimed to encourage saving, investment, and economic growth. Under a consumed-income tax however, that argument is no longer relevant, since the normal return on new saving and investment would be tax-free. Lower tax rates on dividends and capital gains would only provide special tax treatment to the holders of old wealth, allowing them to pay less in taxes on their consumed income than the rest of us. Thus, as I already recommended in chapter 7, the special tax rates on capital gains and dividend income should absolutely be eliminated.[5]

To this list should be added the capital gains tax treatment of "carried interest," which inexplicably did not make the Treasury Department's list of tax expenditures. Carried interest is the share of profits earned by a portfolio investment manager. It is essentially the manager's compensation for managing the fund, and so is no different from a salary or a commission. Logically, carried interest should be taxed exactly the same way as any other form of labor income, and the tax code needs to be changed accordingly.

The next case of special tax treatment involves the interest earned on bonds issued by states, local governments, or several other public or private entities:

- Exclusion of interest on energy facility bonds;
- Exclusion of interest on bonds for water, sewage, and hazardous waste facilities;
- Exclusion of interest on owner-occupied mortgage subsidy bonds;
- Exclusion of interest on rental housing bonds;
- Exclusion of interest on small issue bonds;
- Exclusion of interest on bonds for highway projects and rail-truck transfer facilities;
- Exclusion of interest for airport, dock, and similar bonds;
- Exclusion of interest on student-loan bonds;
- Exclusion of interest on bonds for private nonprofit educational facilities;
- Exclusion of interest on hospital construction bonds;
- Exclusion of interest on veterans housing bonds;
- Exclusion of interest on public purpose state and local bonds; and
- Exclusion of interest on tribal Economic Development Bonds.

All of these exclusions should be eliminated. This is one more example of taxing different forms of income at different rates, in this case at a zero tax rate. Under a consumed-income tax, bondholders' interest income should be taxed when it is consumed, like any other income.

Admittedly, the current exclusion of municipal bond interest lets state and local governments borrow at somewhat lower interest rates. However, as more and more saving has migrated into IRA-type accounts, fewer and fewer investors are willing to accept a lower rate of return on their bonds in return for the tax exemption, and bond ownership is now limited almost solely to the holders of old wealth.

Over time, as the ranks of the old-wealthy grow smaller, municipalities would get a smaller and smaller share of the benefits of this tax treatment, with the remaining larger and larger component accruing to the holders of old wealth. It ultimately doesn't make a lot of sense to create a $10 borrowing subsidy for municipalities by giving wealthy investors a $50 tax break.[6]

Besides, it probably doesn't make a lot of sense to create a borrowing subsidy for municipalities in the first place. States and local governments compete for borrowed funds in the same loan markets as banks, businesses, and other institutional borrowers. Interest rates are the market's mechanism for dividing those loan funds up, for determining who gets to borrow and who doesn't. Having small governments face the same interest rate prices as these other borrowers would lead to more efficient loan markets.[7]

In 2009, provisions were inserted into the tax code that allow some bonds to pay tax credits instead of interest:

- Credit to holders of Gulf and Midwest Tax Credit Bonds;
- Recovery Zone Bonds;
- Credit for holders of zone academy bonds;
- Qualified school construction bonds;
- Qualified energy conservation bonds;
- Build America Bonds.

This "innovation," which as far as I can tell has no logical reason whatsoever to exist, should be eliminated.

As we saw in chapters 5 and 8, borrowing can be treated either of two ways under a consumed-income tax, as taxable (tax the amount borrowed, deduct both the interest and principle repayments) or as nontaxable (do neither). Under current law however, the interest on student loans is deductible:

- Deductibility of student loan interest.

It would make most sense to treat student loans identically to other consumer loans, that is, as nontaxable. Students would not be taxed on the money they borrow to finance their education, nor would they be able to deduct their repayments. That means that the current student loan interest deduction should be eliminated.[8]

Immediate, full elimination of this deduction may not make sense, however. Recent graduates took on these debts, expecting a deduction; normally, our transition rules would "grandfather" these students in, allowing them to continue to deduct their interest over the life of the loans. Also normally, any new loans given to current students would no longer qualify for the deduction.[9]

This disparate treatment of students from a few years ago versus students today may seem unacceptably unfair to most of us. So let me suggest an alternative transition that eliminates the deduction 20 years after the switch to a consumed-income tax is adopted. The most recent graduates at that time would be able to deduct interest for the following 20 years; graduates the next year would get 19 years of deductions, and so on.

It may seem harsh to take away this deduction from young people struggling to pay off their student debt. But supporting education by giving a tax break to student loan interest both encourages excessive borrowing and, worse yet, discourages graduates from paying off their student loans quickly. This is a bad policy approach to the good idea of supporting education.

Besides, there are already better options for providing public assistance to graduates who are excessively burdened with student debt. Various programs for public service workers, employees of nonprofits, low-income area teachers, and members of the military provide loan forgiveness after ten years of payments. Graduates with other low paying jobs are eligible for income-based repayment plans; these individuals are in very low tax brackets and get hardly any assistance from the interest deduction.

Rather, the deduction provides the greatest benefit to recent college graduates with high paying jobs, who are the least burdened by their student loans. Overall, the deduction is just one more example of a poorly designed public subsidy that has survived only because it got itself embedded into our tax system. It needs to be eliminated.

Two additional tax expenditures involve employer-provided insurance:

- Premiums on group term life insurance;
- Premiums on accident and disability insurance.

As we saw in chapter 10, under a consumed-income tax we could either allow a deduction for insurance premiums or then tax insurance payouts, or we could disallow any insurance premiums deduction and not tax insurance payouts. The latter is probably simpler. It is also how we treat any life or disability insurance that you or I purchase. But when our employer pays the premiums, the employer gets a deduction. That asymmetry makes no sense. Rather, the value of those premiums should be included as part of the employee's taxable income on the employee's annual W-2 form.

Finally, one tax expenditure allows businesses to deduct the costs of employee meals and lodging without taxing the employees for these goods:

• Exclusion of employee meals and lodging.

Clearly, meals and lodging are consumption. As I discussed in chapter 8, it makes no sense to allow businesspeople to deduct their meals, just because they happen to conduct business during the meal, since they would have been eating a meal anyway. The same logic applies to employees. Either the cost of the meal should not be deductible for the employer, or the value of the meal should be included as taxable consumed income for the employee.

Lodging, for the businessperson or the employee, is more complicated. I have a home, which I rent or own, and where I usually stay. But on occasion, I need to stay elsewhere for business purposes. For the most part, this is a legitimate business deduction, since the businessperson or employee is getting no additional consumption—a room and a bed—which they wouldn't already have gotten had they been able to stay at home. So as long as the lodging expense is reasonable, it should be deductible as well as excluded from the employee's income.

Eliminating the 30 tax expenditures listed in this section—31, including the carried interest tax expenditure—would reduce the total volume of tax expenditures by about $500 billion per year, or again around 25% of the total. Replacing the mortgage interest deduction with a fixed, refundable tax credit for new homebuyers, as I recommended in chapter 6, might add somewhere around $50 billion back. But we would still be somewhere close to eliminating half of all the tax expenditures at this point—and we still have more to go.

TAX EXPENDITURES FOR
BUSINESSES THAT MUST BE ELIMINATED

As with tax expenditures aimed at individuals, there are a number of tax expenditures aimed at businesses that are entirely inconsistent with either a traditional income tax or a consumed-income tax. The first involved the special treatment of some types of business income:

• Deduction for U.S. production activities.

Once again, income is income is income, regardless of how it is earned. This deduction lowered the effective tax rate on some income earned by some businesses in some industries. It added complexity to the tax code and required complex rules for establishing what was and wasn't qualified production activities income, all to justify who got the 3% more favorable tax treatment and who didn't. If we had to nominate a poster child for what's wrong with our current tax code, this would have been my nominee.

Under a consumed-income tax, we tax all income when it is consumed. The only reason for taxing some consumed income more than other consumed income is to maintain tax progressivity: because I earn more and spend more than you, I can afford to be taxed at a higher rate. There is neither need nor room for the kinds of arcane distinctions that this deduction required.

However, we no longer have to worry about getting rid of this tax expenditure, because it was eliminated as part of the Tax Cuts and Jobs Act (TCJA) enacted in December 2017. Unfortunately, it was replaced by something even worse—but that is a topic I'll get to when we discuss the TCJA in chapter 13.

Two tax expenditures give special tax treatment to oil, gas, and mineral producers:

- Excess of percentage over cost depletion, fuels;
- Excess of percentage over cost depletion, nonfuel minerals.

Rather than have these producers depreciate their investments over a fixed time period, as all other producers do, our current tax code allows oil, gas, and mineral producers to deduct a certain percentage of their gross income. The idea is that the investments depreciate at the rate at which the oil in the well or mineral in the mine is depleted. Which is fine, except that these producers are allowed to take "excess" depletion allowances. That is, suppose I invested $1 million in my oil well, in buying the mineral rights, drilling the well, and so on. Suppose that as I pump and sell my oil, my depletion allowances, based on the income my well generates, total $50,000 a year. Then after 20 years, I will have been allowed to deduct the entire $1 million investment. However, current tax law allows me to continue to take that $50,000 a year deduction for years to come, as long as the well continues to produce. Hence, I'm allowed to deduct depreciation allowances that far exceed my actual investment.

Under my recommended tax rules, that $1 million investment would be expensed, so this provision would be superfluous for new investment. However, all old investments would continue to get special tax treatment that in many cases would be more favorable than that given to new investment. That makes no sense whatsoever. Rather, owners of these old investments should be allowed to continue to take their depletion allowances, but only until their actual past investments have been fully depreciated.[10]

Eliminating these three tax expenditures, along with the 68 previous ones, would remove about 60% of all the special tax provisions from our tax code. We would then have a system that, as a general rule, taxes all income in the same way, regardless of its source, taxing that income when it is consumed.

TAX EXPENDITURES WORTH KEEPING

As I noted at the beginning of this chapter, not all tax expenditures are bad. In a number of cases, some are reasonable ways to achieve appropriate public policy goals. The following are the ones that in my opinion should definitely be kept as part of our tax code.

Two existing tax expenditures help families to invest in higher education:

• Tax credits and deductions for post-secondary education expenses; and
• Parental personal exemption for students age 19.

The existing tax credits and deductions for post-secondary education tuition should be retained, and indeed expanded. Education is an investment; since its payoff, higher future income, is taxed, a deduction or tax credit for its purchase is appropriate under a consumed-income tax. Essentially, that gives educational investments the same tax treatment as investments in business plant and equipment, that is, as a traditional IRA.

Under current law, you can take up to a $2,500 tax credit, for tuition and other qualified educational costs. This credit should be retained, and indeed expanded. On average, the cost of a year's education at a public 4-year university is around $9,000, and at a public community college about $5,000; raising the tax credit limit to somewhere in that range would provide a reasonable tax break for those investing in human capital, in a way that would be reasonably consistent with the tax treatment of other forms of investment under a consumed-income tax.[11]

The parental exemption for students over age 18 recognizes that many full-time students investing in higher education are still financially dependent on their families. It reasonably allows the parents, rather than the student, to use that exemption in calculating their taxes.

Three tax expenditures are related to the existing charitable contribution deduction:

• Charitable contributions to educational institutions;
• Deductibility of charitable contributions, other than education and health; and
• Deductibility of charitable contributions to health institutions.

The deduction should be retained. For the most part, charitable contributions do not represent the donor's consumption. The contributions may represent consumption on the part of the recipient. But generally, that would be for medical or educational services that would be given favorable tax treatment, for religious services that most of us would probably not count as "consumption," or for social services provided to low-income households that would be taxed at a zero rate.

However, the charitable contribution deduction could be considered an attempt to subsidize charitable donations, rather than as a decision that the outlay is not consumption. If the subsidy motive is the correct description of why we give special treatment to charitable contributions, converting the deduction to a refundable tax credit would be appropriate. Either tax treatment would be compatible with a consumed-income tax.

The existing tax expenditures related to childcare should be retained:

* Employer-provided child care exclusion;
* Employer-provided child care credit; and
* Credit for child and dependent care expenses.

For many parents, the high cost of childcare presents a significant hurdle against entering the workforce. At least one parent must choose between staying at home, and providing the childcare herself, or working and using the earned income to pay someone else to provide childcare services. Only if this parent's after-tax earnings are high enough does the working choice make sense.

Any income tax will exacerbate this hurdle. Since the earning-and-purchasing child-care option is taxed and the staying-home option isn't, any tax on earnings will distort this choice in favor of the staying home option. Both the existing child care credit for families that themselves pay for child care, and the tax breaks to employers who provide their employees with free day care, reduce the size of this distortion, by offsetting some of the taxes on this parent's income. Although this tax credit is not in any way integral to the idea of a consumed-income tax, it is a reasonable way to reduce the labor market effects of income taxation, and should be retained.

Two existing tax expenditures are particularly targeted at the working poor:

* Earned income tax credit (EITC); and
* Child credit.

The EITC is a fully refundable tax credit, while the child credit is partly refundable; both help offset the payroll taxes that low-income workers must pay, and increase their incentive to work and support themselves and their families. Both should be retained.

One existing tax expenditure is essentially a tax break for the elderly:

• Social Security benefits for retired and disabled workers and spouses, dependents and survivors.

From society's perspective, the Social Security system is primarily a transfer of funds from the working age population to those elderly. From the individual's perspective however, it might be seen as a type of retirement savings account. While young, I deposit into the system; when old, I withdraw out of it. From the latter perspective, Social Security could be interpreted as another form of IRA, so for tax purposes, it could be treated either as a traditional IRA or as a Roth IRA.

In fact, currently it's treated as both. The Social Security taxes that are withheld from your paycheck are not deductible, so that "contribution" into Social Security is given Roth IRA treatment. But you don't pay income taxes on the matching amount that is paid in your name by your employer. So that contribution into Social Security is treated the same as your employer's contribution into a pension fund, that is, as a traditional IRA. Logically then, under a consumed-income tax, since exactly half your contribution into Social Security gets traditional IRA treatment, exactly one half of your withdrawal from the Social Security system should also get traditional IRA treatment, and be taxed.

That's not even close to how our current income tax treats Social Security income. For many people—those whose non-Social Security income plus half their Social Security income is below $32,000—our current income tax doesn't tax any of those benefits at all. But many people are taxed on at least a portion of their Social Security benefits, and for a small group—those whose non-Social Security income is more than about $37,000 greater than half their Social Security income—85% of their benefits are currently taxed.

None of this current tax treatment makes any particular sense under a consumed-income tax. However, this treatment is not like deducting mortgage interest or not taxing inheritances, both of which would severely violate the logic of a consumed-income tax, and create severe problems in maintaining a consistent tax system.

Leaving the current tax treatment of Social Security benefits unchanged would treat the elderly with low incomes somewhat more favorably than everyone else, and treat the elderly who are well off somewhat less favorably than everyone else. And since discretion is often the better part of valor—or so Shakespeare had the cowardly Falstaff claim—I would suggest that the current tax provisions be maintained under a consumed-income tax.

Finally, one existing tax expenditure probably could have been listed as a tax expenditure that would be normalized if we switched to a consumed-income tax:

• Capital gains exclusion on home sales.

If you recall from chapter 6, under a consumed-income tax owner-occupied housing should be treated like any other consumer durable, with no deduction for the cost of purchasing it, and no tax on the consumption stream it provides. Selling a home means selling the rest of that consumption stream, so in a sense, none of the capital gains on the sale of owner-occupied housing should be taxable.

That would however ignore two issues. One involves windfall gains. Some houses appreciate enormously, because the market changes dramatically. As a result, the owners are prospectively able to take out tax-free a lot more consumption than what they originally purchased. The other involves house flippers, who buy run down homes, put a lot of time and effort into fixing them up, and sell them at a profit—much of which is really their labor income. Allowing them to sell the home tax-free would allow them to escape the tax on labor income that the rest of us have to pay.

The existing capital gains exclusion on home sales is perhaps a reasonable way to handle these two issues. It lets a married couple exclude $500,000 in capital gains, far more than most of us will ever get, but does impose a tax on those lucky few who get that large a gain. In addition, the exclusion is only available if the property has been your principle residence for at least two out of the last five years, which would exclude anyone who makes house flipping a full-time enterprise. So this tax provision should be kept, as is.

Together, these twelve tax expenditures average roughly $230 billion per year, a mere 12% of the current total. Four additional tax expenditures are related to medical care:

• Exclusion of employer contributions for medical insurance premiums and medical care;
• Self-employed medical insurance premiums;
• Deductibility of medical expenses; and
• Distributions from retirement plans for premiums for health and long-term care insurance.

These are reasonable and probably politically untouchable, and average roughly an additional $330 billion per year, about 17% of the current total. That leaves an additional 81 tax expenditures, some probably good (the adoption credit), and others questionable (special rules for certain film and TV production), that together average about $140 billion a year, or around 8% of the current total. Probably, some of these should be kept, and others eliminated, although it may be a challenge determining which are wheat and which are chaff, but even if this group is left untouched, the reforms I'm recommending would move us a considerable distance in cleaning out the special tax provisions from our tax system.

In summary, the tax expenditure changes I recommend are:

1. Give all consumer debt reverse-Roth (nontaxable) treatment
   - Eliminate the mortgage interest deduction for new mortgages;
   - Eliminate the deduction of student loan interest payments, 20 years after enactment.
2. Expense new capital investment
   - Increase the cap on the tuition tax credit, to perhaps $9,000.
3. Eliminate special tax treatments
   - Tax dividend and capital gains income earned outside of tax-deferred savings accounts at the same tax rate as other consumed income;
   - Eliminate the exemption of municipal bond interest income;
   - Eliminate provisions that allow some bonds to pay tax credits;
   - Tax employer-paid insurance premiums as consumed income;
   - Cap depletion allowances at the value of actual past investments.
4. Adopt worldwide sales apportionment:
   - Eliminate the inventory property sales source rules exception;
   - Eliminate the deferral of income from controlled foreign corporations;
   - Eliminate the deferral of taxes for financial firms on certain income earned overseas.
5. Other:
   - Eliminate provisions that have become superfluous due to the other tax changes;
   - Eliminate the exclusion of employee meals.

NOTES

1. U.S. Treasury Department (2017).

2. However, the Treasury's baseline does deviate from the ideal traditional income tax in a number of ways, most importantly by assuming capital gains income is only taxable when it is realized. If the Treasury's baseline stuck more closely to the ideal, the failure to tax capital gains as they accrue would have to be listed as one of the largest tax expenditures.

3. One can argue that education is partly consumption and partly investment. This is probably true for an undergraduate college education, but is far less likely to be true for the kind of education that employers are willing to finance.

4. Assets held within IRAs can be sold, and the proceeds reinvested within the IRA, with no tax consequences. Under the recommended reforms, business assets (like machinery) would be expensed when they are purchased; if they were sold, the

sale price would be taxable income, but if the sale proceeds were used to purchase some other piece of equipment, the expensing of that equipment would offset the taxable income. Finally, for old-wealth financial assets held outside of IRAs, I've recommended that capital gains be rolled over if the sale proceeds are re-invested into other financial assets.

5. See also note 100 in chapter 7 on the "double taxation" of this income.

6. It also doesn't make a lot of sense for state and municipal governments to turn around and give this special tax treatment to private firms and individuals. But that is exactly what they've been doing, since at least the 1980s (Steuerle, 2004, 111–12).

7. Plus, if my experience serving two terms on my local city council is at all typical, local governments rely too much on borrowing. It makes perfect sense for you or I, with our $40,000 or $80,000 annual budgets, to use debt to finance a new car. It makes far less sense for a city with a $5 million budget that purchases new police cars, pickup trucks, and other vehicles on an annual basis, to borrow money for these purchases. If we quit using our tax code to subsidize municipal debt, perhaps local governments would move to wean themselves from unnecessary borrowing.

8. I am not suggesting that we reduce the federal support we provide for post-secondary education. On the contrary, as discussed below, that support should be increased.

9. This is another example of a transition issue, which were addressed in chapter 7.

10. The undepreciated value of the investments should be carried forward at the risk free interest rate, as described in chapter 8.

11. Prior to 2016, a deduction for up to $4,000 in college tuition was available. Both tax treatments—the deduction being more consistent with the "investment" viewpoint, the credit more consistent with the "subsidize education" viewpoint, and more favorable to low-income households are reasonable. The logic of a consumed-income tax suggests that *all* tuition costs should be deductible. However, unless the tuition tax credit were also increased substantially, this would disproportionately favor the children of high-income, high tax bracket households over those from families of more modest means. Hence my suggestion to increase the tuition tax credit to a level that reflects a "typical" cost of education.

Chapter Thirteen

The Trump Tax Cut

The last 12 chapters have identified a sensible and relatively achievable way to reform our current tax system, with as little disruption as possible. After the consumed-income tax was selected as the appropriate target, we examined a variety of tax provisions, seeking out those that fit well together. The result would leave us with a cohesive, coherent tax system. That is how tax reform should be done.

This chapter looks at how not to approach tax reform. In particular, it focuses on the "Tax Cuts and Jobs Act" (TCJA) that Pres. Donald Trump signed into law in December 2017. Appropriately, the law's title did not include the word "reform." A true tax reform would make our tax system more coherent; TCJA did just the opposite, adding arbitrary distinctions to the tax code that are certain to increase the amount of tax gaming that occurs.[1] In this chapter I want to focus on the most important changes, and evaluate their impacts on our tax system.

Let me begin by noting that the first half of the act's title is undisputedly accurate: the act resulted in a huge tax cut, primarily for corporate shareholders and high-income taxpayers, and a corresponding huge increase in the Federal deficit. Whether it will also be a jobs act is very much in question. After all, the U.S. unemployment rate had already fallen to 4.1%, or roughly full employment, at the time it was enacted. And you can count me among those who are highly skeptical about the claims that it will dramatically increase economic growth.

I will begin with a good change included in the TCJA, and then look at several that were far less laudable.

THE GOOD: ENLARGING
THE STANDARD DEDUCTION

This was perhaps the most creative part of the TCJA. The standard deduction was close to doubled in size, but the personal exemptions for both the taxpayers and their dependents were eliminated. In addition, the child tax credit rose by $1,000 per child, which would typically be more beneficial to most households than the personal exemption that was lost. So for most taxpayers who take the standard deduction, this change resulted in a tax cut.

However, households that had previously chosen to itemize their deductions—typically wealthier families—will no longer get the benefits of those personal exemptions, so they faced a tax increase (which for most households was more than offset by other provisions in the act). In addition, many households who previously found it beneficial to itemize deductions would now want to switch from itemizing to taking the standard deduction. These families might or might not benefit from the change, depending on their circumstances.

The overall effect was a slight simplification in our tax system, by reducing the total number of households who itemize their deductions. It was also a slightly progressive change, typically benefiting low-income households more than high-income households. And it was roughly revenue neutral. My grade: A.

THE SO-SO: INVESTMENT
EXPENSING/INTEREST DEDUCTIONS LIMIT

Expensing, that is, the immediate deduction of the full cost of new investment, is as we have seen a key component of a consumed-income tax. Prior to the TCJA, there were two provisions that allowed businesses to partially expense some investments: Section 179, first created in 1958, targeted small businesses, and "bonus depreciation," first created in 2002, aimed at large businesses. Bonus depreciation was due to expire after 2019.

The TCJA expanded both provisions. The Section 179 investment limits were doubled, and the list of qualifying types of investment was expanded slightly. Bonus depreciation was extended through 2022, and increased to full expensing, with a gradual phase out by 2027; here too the list of qualifying types of investment was expanded slightly.

Although I have been recommending that we adopt full expensing throughout this book, this was not the way to do it. Special tax treatment for some kinds of investments but not others, for some size businesses and not others, and for some years at one level but for other years at a different level is no way to run a tax system. It adds complexity, and only assures that tax accountants will be kept plenty busy.

Although a small step was taken toward limiting business interest deductions, that step, a limit of interest deductions to 30% of a business' taxable income, was woefully inadequate. It still leaves in place a bias in the tax code that favors debt over equity in financing investment, and encourages individuals to play untaxed-investment-but-tax-deductible-debt games that a clean tax code would have eliminated.

On the positive side, these changes were revenue increasing, with the revenue gains from the interest deduction limit more than offsetting the revenue losses from the two expensing provisions. And they did somewhat narrow the differences in the tax treatment of different kinds of investments, and in the tax treatment of debt- and equity-financed investment.[2] My grade: B.

THE BAD: CORPORATE TAX "REFORM"

As we saw in chapter 11, under the worldwide corporate tax system we had in place in 2017 an American corporation was taxed on all of its profits, whether they were generated here or abroad, but the American subsidiary of a foreign corporation was taxed only on the profits its earned in the U.S. This gave U.S. firms an incentive to relocate their headquarters overseas.[3] This often occurred through a "corporate inversion," that is, by having a small foreign corporation "buy" its much larger American counterpart using a complex accounting sleight-of-hand.

In contrast, a territorial system will only tax corporations on the profits they earn in the U.S. regardless of whether they are American or foreign corporations. Thus, switching to a territorial system eliminates the perverse incentive to relocate abroad—definitely a good thing. But how you switch matters a lot.

The TCJA began by exempting from taxation the dividends that U.S. corporations received from their foreign subsidiaries, creating a territorial system and solving the inversion problem. But that only widened the door for moving profits overseas, through transfer pricing and the relocation of patents and other intellectual property—definitely not a good idea. So the TCJA added a carrot to encourage corporations to earn their intangible—that is, intellectual property—income here in the U.S., and a stick to penalize corporations whose foreign subsidiaries earn a lot of intellectual property income abroad.

The carrot was the 13.125% tax rate on Foreign-Derived Intangible Income (FDII). U.S. Corporations that export their products and earn profits abroad can attribute a share of those profits to FDII, and have that share taxed at this lower tax rate. Beside the fact that this was probably an export subsidy that violates World Trade Organization (WTO) rules,[4] and can prospectively be gamed,[5] it was also a special low tax rate on infra-marginal returns. But as we saw in chapters 5 and 11, infra-marginal returns are the result of special circumstances that are particularly likely to accrue to large corporations. Unlike taxing work or the normal returns to saving and investing, taxing infra-marginal returns results in little to no economic distortion whatsoever, so this is exactly the income that should be taxed at the highest rate. Instead, as a way to induce corporations to relocate this income to the U.S., the TCJA taxes it at an extremely low rate—only slightly higher than the tax rate on a wage-earning household with a $40,000 a year combined income.

The stick was a minimum tax on "Global Intangible Low-Taxed Income" (GILTI). This was supposed to be a tax on the profits earned by foreign subsidiaries on their intellectual property. However, the TCJA measures that taxable GILTI by taking all the earnings of foreign subsidiaries and subtracting a 10% return on the subsidiary's tangible assets—things like its buildings and equipment. As Kamin et al. note (2017a, 2017b), this gives U.S. corporations an incentive to invest (and create jobs) outside the U.S., because any additional tangible assets owned by the foreign subsidiary will likely reduce the corporation's GILTI tax.[6] Note also that with the GILTI tax, we are back to taxing worldwide income, so the "corporate inversion" incentive is back on the table. It is however reduced, since the GILTI tax rate is only 10.5%.

To top this all off, the TCJA cut the corporate tax rate by two-fifths, from 35% down to 21%. As I discussed in chapter 11, the problem with the corporate income tax was not that the rate was too high, but that the tax was, and still is, very poorly designed. Moving to full cash flow treatment (by expensing all new investment and disallowing interest deductions on new business loans) plus adopting sales-apportionment would result in a well-designed tax purely on excess, above-normal profits. Since it would tax only excess profits, there would be no need, or justification, for reducing the tax rate. Besides, most multinational corporations doing business in the U.S. are partly or fully owned by foreigners. So cutting the corporate income tax rate gave a substantial tax windfall to wealthy foreigners.

Moving to cash-flow treatment would be revenue increasing over a 20 year horizon. Sales-apportionment would likely also be revenue increasing.[7] Thus, my proposed corporate tax changes would not have increased federal deficits, but could be used either to shrink those deficits, or to reduce individual tax rates, or both. In contrast, the TCJA corporate tax rate reduction alone has blown an enormous hole in the federal budget, increasing federal deficits by $1.5 trillion over the next 10 years. My grade: D.

THE UGLY: SPECIAL TAX
TREATMENT OF PASS-THROUGH BUSINESSES

Let's make this perfectly clear: it is a bad idea to have one tax rate for one form of income, and a different tax rate for another form of income. The reason it's a bad idea involves tax accountants and tax lawyers, who, when given the opportunity, will discover a creative way to turn the higher taxed income into the lower taxed income. The poster child for tax avoidance is "carried interest." This is essentially the income hedge fund managers earn by managing a hedge fund. Using creative contract provisions, tax lawyers and accountants have turned this salary income into capital gains income. As a result, carried interest is taxed at substantially lower rates than ordinary income.

The TCJA lets some, but not all, small businesses and S-corporations earn 20% of their income tax-free. The deduction is limited for some types of businesses (law and accounting firms) but not others (engineering firms), so it creates a game of turn-this-kind-of-income-into-that-kind-of-income. For example, in some industries, if a worker can switch from being an employee to an independent contractor (and hence a small business), voila, 20% of his or her income would become tax-free. A medical practice that owns their own building can create a Real Estate Investment Trust (REIT), sell their building to the REIT, and then rent the building from themselves. Then 20% of the rent the REIT earns would be tax-free. Undoubtedly there are other games to be discovered, and enterprising tax accountants and tax lawyers are sharpening their pencils in pursuit of new loopholes for their clients to wiggle through.[8]

If you love tax loopholes, you should absolutely love this TCJA provision. I don't, so my grade: F–.

THE SUM OF THE PARTS

Hopefully this book has helped you come to see that a good tax system is not just a random collection of tax provisions combined into a single tax code. In a good tax system, all of its provisions are consistent with a single organizing principle that ensures that all those provisions fit together into a logical, coherent whole.

So what is the organizing principle behind the TCJA? As far as I can tell, there is only one common thread: these provisions, as a whole, dramatically reduce the tax liabilities of very high-income households. In particular, the special tax treatment of pass-through businesses primarily benefits households in the top 10%. The reduction in the corporate tax rate also disproportionately benefits the very wealthy.

Now, maybe it is true that high-income households are currently overtaxed, and maybe it isn't true. But a proposal just to reduce their tax burden, while adding $1.5 trillion to our national debt, is tax reallocation, not tax reform. We all, Democrat, Independent, or Republican, right or left, agree that our tax system is a mess and needs fixed. A true tax reform would address those concerns, not necessarily in a way that would satisfy any one political perspective, but certainly in a way that all sides would agree is measured and reasonable and rational.

From that perspective, the TCJA utterly failed at achieving anything even approaching true tax reform. My overall grade: F.

The TCJA-related tax changes I recommend are:

1. Adopt worldwide sales apportionment:
   • Eliminate the special tax treatments of FDII and GILTI.
2. Eliminate special tax treatments:
   • Eliminate the 20% exclusion of pass-through business income.

NOTES

1. Kamin et al. (2017a, 2017b).
2. Gravelle and Marples (2018, tables 1, 2).
3. Technically, the location of the headquarters itself, where the CEO works and the board of directors meet, need not change. Rather, for tax purposes the location of the "parent company" changes. However, this is often loosely described as headquarters relocation.
4. Avi-Yonah and Vallespinos (2018). Admittedly, even if the EU lodges a complaint with the WTO, and the WTO upholds their complaint, the U.S. could ignore the WTO ruling. But that would likely start a trade war with Europe, and contrary to what you've heard, trade wars are not "easy to win." Indeed, as the trade war set off by the Smoot-Hawley tariffs in 1930 demonstrated, in a trade war there are no winners.
5. Kamin et al. (2017b).
6. Kamin et al. (2017b) note that if these foreign assets are purchased by borrowing, both the interest cost and the 10% return could be deducted from the GILTI tax, giving the corporation two ways to cut its taxes by investing abroad.
7. Avi-Yonah et al. (2009).
8. Kamin et al. (2017a, 2017b).

Chapter Fourteen

Summary

The Needed Tax Changes

We've seen thus far that, to make sense, we need a tax system that is coherent and consistent with some logical principle, whether the principle of a traditional income tax or of a consumed-income tax. That would eliminate the inconsistencies within our current tax system that add complexity and create unfairness and opportunities for tax shelters.

We've also seen that a consistent, coherent traditional income tax is for all practical purposes unattainable. But moving to a consistent, coherent consumed-income tax would not be particularly difficult. We have after all been evolving in this direction since at least 1974, when Congress created the IRA. A sensible tax reform would only need to complete this evolution.

We've also seen that, to be attainable, tax reform needs to be as minimally disruptive as possible. Most tax changes have transition effects that either suddenly burden taxpayers who were previously untaxed, or suddenly provide a windfall gain to taxpayers who had expected to have to pay some tax liability. In both cases, these tax changes can be seen as unfair, and therefore undesirable. And all tax changes create political opposition from those who are asked to shoulder a greater tax burden. Ideally then, tax reform would involve as few changes as possible, just enough to create consistency without engendering much disruption.

But as we've also seen, that is exactly what moving to a consistent, coherent progressive consumed-income tax would entail. It would require a relatively small number of changes in our tax code. Some of them might spur considerable controversy, but for most individuals, the changes would not be earth shattering.

Although I would like to believe that you have agreed with all of my recommendations, realistically that is extremely unlikely. So the question that remains is, to what extent can we as a society feel free to pick and choose, adopting some of these changes but not others? Which changes are most critical to a coherent tax system, and which are the least necessary?

To help answer these questions, in this chapter I will summarize all of the recommended changes, and divide them into seven groups, rated from Most Critical down to Appropriate. Any reform effort that is unwilling to adopt the critical changes will leave us with a mess not unlike the one we already have. Any reform that picks and chooses from the last few groups will be, in my opinion, less than complete, but would at least represent a significant step forward. And so, the seven groups:

GROUP 1: MOST CRITICAL—
GIVE DEBT NONTAXABLE TREATMENT

The most critical of the changes mentioned in the previous chapters would eliminate the biggest inconsistency of all: our simultaneously favorable tax treatments of both saving and borrowing. It makes absolutely no sense to have a tax code that simultaneously reward those who save and those who borrow. Since the favorable tax treatment of saving is fundamental to a consumed-income tax, the favorable tax treatment of borrowing absolutely must go:

- Eliminate the mortgage interest deduction for new mortgages;
- Convert the mortgage interest deduction for old mortgages into a tax credit, to be phased out over 20 years;
- Eliminate the deduction of student loan interest payments, 20 years after enactment;
- Eliminate the interest deduction for new business debt (including corporate debt);
- Allow the continued deduction of interest on old business loans, provided they continue to be paid off in a timely fashion.

None of these changes would be politically popular, but again, they are absolutely critical to creating a tax system that actually makes sense. The political temptation would be to skip these unpopular changes, while enacting the more popular ones that follow. So let me create my Rule of Tax Knavery: any tax reform proposal that fails to address the existing tax subsidies to borrowing is nothing more than pure political fraud.

GROUP 2: NECESSARY—TAX SHELTERING SAVINGS

The second group of changes would loosen the restrictions on IRA-type saving, allowing the vast majority of new saving to be deposited in these types of accounts. These changes would expand on the existing features in our tax code that give consumption-tax treatment to certain types of saving, while combining and simplifying those features into a single coherent tax treatment:

- Raise the annual contribution limits on tax-deferred savings accounts to $50,000;
- Eliminate all penalties on early (i.e., pre-retirement) withdrawals;
- Eliminate all required rates of withdrawal;
- Eliminate redundant savings accounts (e.g., MSAs, ESAs);
- Allow the portion of the sale of a business taxed as ordinary income to be rolled over into an IRA.

GROUP 3: NECESSARY—EXPENSING INVESTMENT

The third group of changes would allow all new investment to be immediately expensed, consistent with the logic of taxing income only when it is consumed:

- Allow new capital equipment to be immediately and fully expensed (or depreciated over its lifetime, with the undepreciated value carried forward at the risk-free interest rate);
- Allow the continued deductible depreciation of business and corporate assets purchased before the tax change;
- Allow the purchaser of a business to expense the portion of the sale of a business taxed as ordinary income for the seller;
- Increase the cap on the tuition tax credit, to perhaps $9,000.

These changes to the tax treatment of savings and investments would be especially popular among those who feel that saving and investing is currently overtaxed. These changes should absolutely *not* be adopted without also addressing the existing tax treatment of debt. Otherwise, these changes would make our tax system less coherent rather than more coherent.

All of the above changes would be fundamental to completing the conversion of our tax system to a consumed-income tax. The next few changes would make out tax code better conform to the logic of a consumed-income tax: tax all income, when that income is consumed.

GROUP 4: LOGICAL—TREAT INHERITANCES AS INCOME

The fourth group of changes would give inheritances the same treatment as other forms of income, while allowing them to be fully deposited into IRAs:

- Tax inheritances and large gifts as income;
- Allow inherited cash and financial assets and large financial gifts to be fully deposited into an IRA;
- Allow a lifetime $10,000 exemption on inherited household goods;
- Allow the tax on inherited consumer durables to be paid over a 30 year period, with interest;
- Modify the estate tax to reduce tax avoidance;
- Allow previously expensed inherited business assets to be expensed;
- Allow the continued deductible depreciation of not fully depreciated inherited business assets purchased before the tax change.

GROUP 5: LOGICAL—LIMIT ROTH IRAS

The fifth group of changes would restrict Roth IRAs to conform to the consumed-income tax logic, and ensure that infra-marginal returns do not go untaxed:

- Limit Roth IRAs to holding low risk securities like FDIC insured money market accounts;
- Automatically classify FDIC insured savings and checking accounts as Roth IRAs;
- Cap total Roth IRA assets at $250,000;
- Grandfather existing Roth IRAs assets, but require any new deposits, account earnings, and asset exchanges to meet the new tax rules;
- Allow lump sum insurance payouts under some circumstances to be fully deposited into "insurance" Roth IRAs, with temporarily high Roth IRA caps;
- Allow small businesses to hold cash balances (up to some limit) in Roth-IRA accounts.

Together, these five groups of changes would allow almost everyone to be taxed only when they consumed their income, rather than when they earned it. All savings and investing eligible for IRA treatment would be taxed identically, sharply reducing the economic inefficiency that our current tax system creates. The tax code would treat both saving and borrowing consistently.

And consumed wealth would be taxed the same, whether that wealth was earned or whether it had been inherited.

GROUP 6: APPROPRIATE—ELIMINATE SPECIAL TAX TREATMENTS

The sixth group of changes, while not absolutely necessary for a consumed-income tax system to be adopted, would be highly appropriate. They would allow us to eliminate a variety of special tax treatments that have little to no economic justification, both to limit abuse and to make them more consistent with the rest of the tax code:

- Tax dividends and capital gains held outside of tax-deferred savings accounts at the same tax rate as other consumed income;
- Allow capital gains to be rolled over into new investments, but only allow capital losses to offset realized capital gains;
- Tighten the rules on the deduction of "business" consumption;
- Tax employer-paid insurance premiums as consumed income;
- Eliminate the exemption of municipal bond interest income;
- Eliminate provisions that allow some bonds to pay tax credits;
- Eliminate the 20% exclusion of pass-through business income;
- Cap depletion allowances at the value of actual past investments;
- Eliminate the exclusion of employee meals.

GROUP 7: APPROPRIATE—ADOPT WORLDWIDE SALES APPORTIONMENT

The seventh group of changes would, along with the expensing of new corporate investment and the changes to the tax treatment of corporate debt, convert the corporate income tax into a tax on all above-normal corporate profits generated in the U.S.:

- Tax a share of corporate worldwide profits, based on the share of its sales located in the U.S.;
- Eliminate the inventory property sales source rules exception;
- Eliminate the deferral of income from controlled foreign corporations;
- Eliminate the deferral of taxes for financial firms on certain income earned overseas;
- Eliminate the special tax treatments of FDII and GILTI.

I would note that, since the corporate income tax would tax only above-normal corporate profits, there would be no justification for taxing it at anything less than the highest personal tax rate.

OTHER REASONABLE CHANGES

The final three changes would be entirely optional. The first would just clean up the tax code, eliminating special provisions for certain groups that would be superfluous. These provisions would become available to everyone under a consumed-income tax. The second would allow businesses to carry forward their tax losses with interest, again at the risk-free interest rate. Assuming that we adopt the provision allowing unused depreciation allowances to be carried forward with interest, it would seem odd if any other costs that the firm is forced to carry forward were not also given this tax treatment.

Finally, the third change, while entirely optional from an economic viewpoint, is probably mandatory from a political viewpoint. We cannot create a coherent tax system without eliminating the mortgage interest deduction. But politically, that's a total nonstarter, unless we have some other tax break to home ownership to replace it. There are a number of options, but the first-time homebuyer refundable tax credit is the one that makes most sense.

- Eliminate provisions that have become superfluous due to the other tax changes;
- Allow tax losses to be carried forward at the risk-free interest rate;
- Provide new, first-time homebuyers with a fixed, refundable tax credit.

So that's it—seven groups of critical to appropriate changes to our tax code, with a handful of additional options. This is a tax reform that's actually achievable.

One other change, that I have not specified, would be some appropriate adjustment in tax rates. I have not even considered attempting to figure out what those rate changes would need to be, for two reasons. First, coming up with an appropriate pattern of tax brackets that would continue to raise some required amount of tax revenue is way too complicated. But that's why we have the Congressional Budget Office, to run all the complex simulations needed to make that determination.

Second, it is in general a bad idea to start with some pre-determined set of tax rates, and then design the tax code around those rates. That is putting the cart before the horse. It's far better to begin with a set of tax provisions that makes sense, a revenue target that adequately funds the federal budget, and a desired degree of progressivity. Then you solve the complicated math problem to find out what pattern of tax rates accomplishes all your other goals. One of the problems with the TCJA was that the Republicans began with a predetermined corporate tax rate of 20%, and a predetermined revenue loss of $1.5 trillion over 10 years, and then started adding and subtracting other tax changes to make the whole thing fit. Not surprisingly, when you first buy the piece of material and then design the dress to fit it, the result will not exactly be a thing of beauty.

In general, I suspect that if we wish to keep the same level of tax progressivity that we had in 2017, the rate structure would also be very similar to what we currently had then.[1] Some of the changes listed above, most notably the raised IRA contribution limits and the full expensing of new investment, would be revenue losing in the first few years.[2]

But other changes, principally the elimination of the mortgage interest deduction, taxing inheritances, and taxing dividends and capital gains at the ordinary income tax rate, would be revenue increasing (although the capital gains rollover provision would somewhat offset that). As a ballpark estimate, my guess is that the revenue increases and revenue decreases would roughly balance out. If not, tax rates should be adjusted appropriately.

NOTES

1. As Steuerle (2004, 51) shows, the overall progressivity of the personal income tax did not change dramatically between 1979 and 2001. An update through 2013 in Congressional Budget Office (2016) shows that overall progressivity has continued to be stable over the last two decades. Maintaining roughly that same level of progressivity makes sense.

2. Essentially, both provisions allow more tax deductions now, and fewer later. The immediate impact would be a loss in tax revenue. However, over time the higher-deductions-now from this year's savings and investment would be mostly offset by the lower-deductions-now on previous years' savings and investment, and the revenue loss would approach zero.

Chapter Fifteen

Is Reform Attainable?

In the previous 14 chapters I've laid out a tax reform designed to make our tax system consistent, coherent, and somewhat simpler. It is a tax reform that makes perfect economic sense. But to actually get enacted, it would need to make political sense as well. So in this chapter I'll ask the question, is it feasible in our current political environment?

Any tax reform will create winners and losers. If the winners are particularly numerous, or powerful, or politically favored, their gains may outweigh the losers' losses, and the tax reform may be enacted. On the other hand, if the losers are sufficiently vocal or sufficiently persuasive, they may succeed in blocking the reform. So the first question to explore is, under this tax reform, who would win and who would lose?

Because this tax reform is as minimally disruptive as possible—both by design and because our current system is already not that far from a consumed-income tax—the list of losers is not all that long.

WINNERS

The biggest group of winners is anyone who saves. The recommended reform would simplify life for the vast majority of savers. It would raise the annual ceiling on IRA deposits to much more than they could possibly afford to save. It would allow a single IRA savings account to be used for a variety of purposes. And it would eliminate all mandatory withdrawals, especially after age 70. It would also give Roth IRA treatment to most savings accounts, eliminating the need to report any interest earned on them to the IRS.

Small business owners would also be winners, because the tax reform would simplify life considerably. Tax distinctions between capital assets, inventory, and other purchases would disappear. So would the need to depreciate assets over multiple year periods. Income would be income: distinctions between ordinary income and capital gains income would no longer be relevant. Since the normal return on investment would be effectively untaxed, investment decisions could be made without needing to consider their tax consequences.

Middle class first-time homebuyers would also win. A fixed, refundable tax credit would provide them with much more assistance than the current mortgage interest deduction. The tax credit would broaden the pool of first-time homebuyers, and might well spur more affordable housing in urban markets, that currently squeeze out many prospective homebuyers.

Increasing the cap on the tuition tax credit to around $9,000 would be a big win for college students and their families. Yes, this would fall well short of Bernie Sanders' "free college for all." But in a world where tuition varies widely from one college to the next—and even differs between different public universities within the same state system—it is not clear how Bernie's pledge could be implemented literally. Raising the tuition tax credit cap to around $9,000 would make college much more affordable, and would almost certainly lead to a major increase in our country's annual investment in higher education.

Finally, the U.S. economy as a whole would win. All tax disincentives on savings and investment decisions would disappear, as would all tax distortions that divert investment dollars into relatively low productivity (but highly tax favored) forms of investment. Although I am very skeptical about claims about tax changes spurring economic growth, the simpler, cleaner tax system that I have recommended cannot help but improve our economy's performance, even if that improvement turns out to be only a small one.

Notice that the winners are almost everyone. If our politicians care primarily about the vast majority of Americans, this tax reform could well be a slam-dunk.

LOSERS

Generally, the losers would be those who currently get some special tax treatment that would disappear under the recommended tax reform. There are four such groups.

Borrowers would be the first group to lose under the recommended reforms, because they would lose the ability to deduct their interest payments. That would not affect households with credit card debt, since that interest is already non-deductible. However, it would affect businesses, which typically have lines of credit that they tap into regularly. For most businesses, the benefits of expensing investment would outweigh the costs of losing interest deductibility. But some businesses, particularly those that rely heavily on debt, would be net losers.

But the predictable response to the recommended tax reform—changing how a business is financed, to rely less on debt—would be a win for the economy as a whole. Debt-heavy businesses are often the first to go belly up during an economic downturn. The losses they impose on our financial institutions cause those financial institutions to tighten credit, making the downturn worse. There's a reason that the phrase "financial panic" is a synonym for a recession. If tax reform leads to less debt financing, it will improve our overall economic stability.

Owners of multi-million dollar homes would be the second group to lose under the recommended reforms. As we saw in chapter 6, the benefits of the mortgage interest deduction accrue primarily to high-income households who own large, expensive homes. Eliminating the mortgage interest deduction, even if it's replaced with a first-time-homebuyer tax credit, will hurt these homeowners, both by taking a deduction away from them and by potentially reducing the resale value of their homes. However, this would only affect the high end of the market, since the first-time-homebuyer tax credit would positively affect the rest of the housing market.

The third group to lose would be the owners of old wealth, the primary beneficiaries of Trump's TCJA. Their dividend and capital gains income would no longer be taxed at special, low rates. They would no longer be able to earn tax-free income on municipal bonds. They would no longer be able to exclude 20% of their pass-through business income.

The final group to lose would be any inheritors of old wealth who consume that old wealth. This group currently pays no taxes whatsoever on the wealth they inherit and consume, but are taxed only on any income that wealth earns them. Heirs who consume less than what they earn will be taxed less under the proposed reforms, because those earnings will be tucked away in an IRA. But heirs who spend more than their earnings—that is, if they dip into their inheritance to finance their lifestyle—will be taxed more than under our current tax system. A consumed-income tax is designed to reward saving and investing. If that is appropriate for the vast majority of the population who have to work for the income they can either spend or save, it should be appropriate for the fortunate few who are handed that income through inheritance.

However, middle class inheritors would not lose because of the reforms. Under our current tax system, the elderly are required to make withdrawals from their IRAs, whether they need to spend their savings or not. Their heirs as a result get smaller, already taxed inheritances. The recommended reform would allow the elderly to leave their savings in their IRA, so the heirs will get a somewhat larger, not-yet-taxed inheritance. Those heirs would then pay taxes on that not-yet-taxed inheritance only when they choose to spend it.

Current tax law also requires heirs to make withdrawals from any IRAs they inherit, again whether they need to spend the money of not. The recommended reform would eliminate all required withdrawals. Heirs who inherit an IRA could leave the money untaxed until they need to spend it—one more example of how this tax reform would simplify life a little bit for savers.

So our winners are almost everyone, and the economy as a whole. Our losers are the very wealthy, owners of expensive homes, business owners who heavily rely on debt, and socialite heirs. What does that tell us about this tax reform's political feasibility?

Let me note before I continue that my expertise is in tax policy, not tax politics, so perhaps on this topic, your ability to speculate is as good or even better than mine. But allow me to speculate nonetheless, if only because it will allow me to explore in a bit more detail the policy implications of the recommended tax reform.

DEMOCRATS

Democrats typically argue that our current tax system is unfair, full of loopholes exploited by the wealthy, and not sufficiently progressive. Many of their criticisms of Trump's TCJA were that its tax cuts, both to individuals and to corporations, primarily benefitted the top few percent of the population.

Assuming that they are true to those principles, the reforms recommended in this book should be an easy sell to Democrats. The tax reform's benefits would be widespread, a variety of tax provisions exploited by the wealthy would be eliminated, and tax progressivity could return to the level it was in 2016. True, those too poor to save much would not really benefit from this reform, but they would not be hurt either. And the middle class as a whole would win, at the expense of the very wealthy. So this should be a reform that most Democrats could wholeheartedly embrace.

I noted in chapter 5 that a consumed-income tax levies taxes on inframarginal returns without taxing the normal return to saving. Some Democrats might argue that it is unfair to tax only a part of the return to saving. After all, income from working is fully taxed. But the tax rates on dividends and capital gains—major components of the return to saving—are currently substantially lower than the tax rates on labor income. Certainly a consumed-income tax would tax normal returns less than under current law, but it would also tax infra-marginal returns substantially more than under our current system.

In addition, adopting a consumed-income tax would end the tug-of-war between tax progressivity and saving incentives: a more progressive tax would no longer imply reduced incentives to save and invest. Thus the wealthy could be taxed at significantly higher rates on their above-normal returns, without affecting saving and investment incentives. So over all, a consumed-income tax should be an easy sell to most Democrats.

REPUBLICANS

It is less clear how Republicans would respond to this reform. It would depend on why they currently favor tax cuts.

Recall that under a traditional income, the incentives to save and invest are diametrically opposed to increased tax progressivity. Over the last forty years Republicans have sponsored tax cuts that they justify as pro-growth, but which Democrats deride as tax cuts for the rich: Reagan's "Economic Recovery Tax Act" of 1981, Bush's "Economic Growth and Tax Relief Reconciliation Act" of 2001, Bush's "Jobs and Growth Tax Relief Reconciliation Act" of 2003, and Trump's "Tax Cuts and Jobs Act" of 2017. All of these tax cuts primarily benefitted the wealthy. All were predicted (by their Republican supporters) to increase saving, investment, and economic growth. All led to larger Federal deficits.

When Democrats look at these tax cuts, they point to the benefits they provided to the wealthy, and argue that the Republican's motivation was just to cut taxes on the wealthy. When Republicans look at these tax cuts, they point to the benefits they provided to savers and investors, and argue that their motivation was to increase economic growth.

Many parts of these tax cuts—more rapid depreciation allowances, the expansion of IRA-type savings accounts—have indeed had strong incentive-enhancing aspects. But many—lower tax rates on corporate dividends, lower corporate tax rates, and the TCJA 20% exclusion of pass-through business income—have been primarily tax cuts for owners of existing wealth, with little to no incentive effects. Perhaps the Republican lawmakers who proposed these latter provisions couldn't really distinguish cuts that were primarily incentive-enhancing from cuts that were primarily (or exclusively) wealthy-benefitting. Of course, under the logic of a traditional income tax, there was no real need to make that distinction. But under a consumed-income tax, they would no longer be one and the same.

The tax reform outlined in this book is, as noted in the list of winners and losers, not designed to provide tax cuts to the wealthy. It is however designed to eliminate taxes on the normal return to new savings and investment, giving a potential tax boost to saving, investment, and economic growth. (Again, I suspect that boost will only be small, but if the Republican view is accurate, the economic boost from this reform could be quite large.) So if Republicans are motivated in the way they describe themselves, as pro-growth, this tax reform is one that they too should wholeheartedly embrace. But if Republicans are motivated in the way Democrats describe them, as pro-wealthy, this tax reform is one that they would strongly oppose.

Paradoxically, by giving Republicans everything they say they want—a tax code that has close to zero disincentive effects on saving and investment—the reform would take away from them the issue that has been one of their party's defining features. After all, if the tax code no longer inhibited investment and economic growth, wouldn't there be less reason to cut tax rates dramatically?

My guess is, most Republicans would support this tax reform. After all, it does give them exactly what they have told us many times they want, and I believe most of them do truly want—a pro-growth tax code, that has close to zero disincentive effects on saving and investment.

So is this tax reform feasible? If Democrats were highly likely to support it, and Republicans reasonably likely to support it, then yes it is. But we won't really know unless and until it, or something very much like it, may actually be proposed in Congress.

Chapter Sixteen

Conclusion

I started working on this book in 2012. Paul Ryan's "Path to Prosperity" budget proposal had just come out, with a tax proposal more cutting-taxes-on-the-wealthy than improving-investment-incentives. I had just read Carroll and Viard's newly published book, "Progressive Consumption Taxation," an interesting book, but essentially just another X-tax proposal. It was clear to me that some type of consumption-timed tax was the only logical option. But I had yet to see any proposal that really worked. In particular, nothing I had seen had gotten the transition right. No proposal moved us to a consumption-timed tax without either too much complexity, or handing the wealthy a big tax windfall.

I began writing this not because I thought I had anything new to say, but merely to see if getting the transition right was even possible. It took years, of writing chapters and then laying the work aside, then returning to re-examine this issue or that. Eventually I began to believe that I had stumbled across an actually workable transition. Fortunately this transition was a very simple one, essentially leaving the wealthy in the status quo until they leave their wealth to the next generation.

I believe this book presents the simplest possible way to achieve real tax reform. The cure I've recommended follows directly from the diagnosis: if the problems in our tax system arise first and foremost because of the system's inconsistencies, its lack of cohesion, then we need a tax code that consistently adheres to a single logic. And since adhering to the logic of a traditional income tax is nigh impossible, we should apply the workable logic of a consumed-income tax instead.

The essence of the reform proposal would be to broaden and complete a number of tax code changes that date back to the 1980s, like the creation of the IRA. The most important changes would move almost everyone, all but the very wealthy and the very highly compensated, to a tax system that taxes their income not when they earn it, but when they spend it. That would greatly simplify the tax code for almost everyone, eliminate most tax shelters, and bring about a significantly fairer tax system. All that, from a relatively few fundamental tax code changes.

As noted in chapter 1, from a Democratic perspective tax reform needs to be structured to ensure that the wealthy pay their fair share in taxes. From a Republican perspective, tax reform needs to ensure that the incentives to save and invest are protected. One eminent tax lawyer, noting that this difference in viewpoints has defined the political struggle over taxes spanning the last 30 years, commented that there is "no straightforward way to bridge this philosophical and political gap."[1]

I would like to believe that he was mistaken, that the reforms I recommend do just that. They ensure that at the margin, the return to saving and investing, at both the individual level and the corporate level, are entirely unaffected by the tax system. But they also ensure that the tax code remains progressive, with features such as personal exemptions and the standard deduction, the earned income tax credit, and a series of progressive tax rates.

Of course, there are many things that this reform proposal does not do. It doesn't change the child-care tax credit, the retirement savings contributions credit, or the residential energy credit. It affects neither the child tax credit, nor the earned income tax credit. And it does not change the deduction for charitable contributions. Maybe some of these need to be changed; maybe not. But changing them is not essential to sensible tax reform, so I would recommend leaving them unchanged, at least for now.

I hope this book has convinced you that real, sensible tax reform is at least reasonably possible. Whether following my recommendations or using some similar variant, I believe we need to take the next step, and adopt some form of a progressive consumed-income tax. This book has laid out one potential way of reaching that goal. All we now need is the political will.

NOTE

1. Graetz (1997, 167).

Bibliography

Aaron, Henry J. and Harvey Galper. 1985. *Assessing Tax Reform.* Washington, DC: The Brookings Institute.

Altschuler, Rosanne and Harry Grubert. 2002. "Repatriation Taxes, Repatriation Strategies and Multinational Financial Policy." *Journal of Public Economics* 87: 73–107.

Altshuler, Rosanne and Harry Grubert, 2010. "Formula Apportionment: Is It Better Than the Current System and Are There Better Altenatives?" *National Tax Journal* 63: 1145–1184.

Anderson, John E. and Atrayee Ghosh Roy. 2001. "Eliminating Housing Tax Preferences: A Distributional Analysis." *Journal of Housing Economics* 10: 41–58.

Arena, Matteo P. and Roper, Andrew H. 2010. "The Effect of Taxes on Multinational Debt Location." *Journal of Corporate Finance* 16: 637–654.

Andrews, William D. 1974. "A Consumption-Type or Cash Flow Personal Income Tax." *Harvard Law Review* 87: 1113–1188.

Auerbach, Alan J. and Michael P. Devereux. 2015. "Cash Flow Taxes in an International Setting." Saïd Business School WP 2015-3. https://dx.doi.org/10.2139/ssrn.2556892.

Auerbach, Alan J., Michael P. Devereux and Helen Simpson. 2010. "Taxing Corporate Income." In Institute for Fiscal Studies, *Dimensions of Tax Design,* 837–913. New York, NY: Oxford University Press.

Auerbach, Alan. J. and Laurence J. Kotlikoff. 1983. "National Savings, Economic Welfare, and Structure of Taxation." In Martin Feldman, ed., *Behavioral Simulation Methods in Tax Policy Analysis,* 459–498. Chicago: University of Chicago Press.

Auerbach, Alan. J. and Laurence J. Kotlikoff. 1987. *Dynamic Fiscal Policy.* New York: Cambridge University Press.

Avi-Yonah, Reuven S., Kimberly A. Clausing and Michael C. Durst. 2009. "Allocating Business Profits for Tax Purposes: A Proposal to Adopt a Formulary Profit Split." *Florida Tax Review* 9: 497–553.

Avi-Yonah, Reuven S. and Martin Vallespinos. 2018. "The Elephant Always Forgets: Tax Reform and the WTO." https://dx.doi.org/10.2139/ssrn.3113059.

Bartelsman, Eric J. and Roel M.W.J. Beetsma. 2003. "Why Pay More? Corporate Tax Avoidance through Transfer Pricing in OECD Countries." *Journal of Public Economics* 87: 2225–2252.

Becker, Johannes and Nadine Riedel. 2012. "Cross-Border Tax Effects on Affiliate Investment—Evidence from European Multinationals." *European Economic Review* 56: 436–450.

Binner, Amy and Brett Day. 2015. "Exploring Mortgage Interest Deduction Reforms: An Equilibrium Sorting Model with Endogenous Tenure Choice." *Journal of Public Economics* 122: 40–54.

Boadway, Robin and Neil Bruce. 1984. "A General Proposition on the Design of a Neutral Business Tax." *Journal of Public Economics* 24: 231–239.

Bond, Stephen and Michael P. Devereux. 2002. "Cash Flow Taxes in an Open Economy." CEPR Discussion Paper no. 3401. https://ssrn.com/abstract=319007.

Bourassa, Steven C., Donald R. Haurin, R. Jean Haurin, and Patric H. Hendershott. 1994. "Independent Living and Home-Ownership: An Analysis of Australian Youth." *Australian Economic Review*: 29–44.

Bourassa, Steven C. and Ming Yin. 2008. "Tax Deductions, Tax Credits and the Homeownership Rate of Young Urban Adults in the United States." *Urban Studies* 45: 1141–1161.

Bradford, David F. 1980. "The Case for a Personal Consumption Tax." In Joseph A. Pechman, ed., *What Should Be Taxed: Income or Expenditure? 75–125.* Washington, DC: The Brookings Institute.

Bradford, David F. 1986. *Untangling the Income Tax.* Cambridge, MA: Harvard University Press.

Bradford, David F. 2005. "A Tax System for the Twenty-First Century." In Alan J. Auerbach and Kevin A. Hassett, eds. *Towards Fundamental Tax Reform,* 11–32. Washington, DC: AEI Press.

Bradford, David F. and the U.S. Treasury Tax Policy Staff. 1984. *Blueprints for Basic Tax Reform.* 2nd ed. Arlington, VA: Tax Analysts.

Carroll, Robert and Alan D. Viard. 2012. *Progressive Consumption Taxation: The X Tax Revisited.* Washington, DC: AEI Press.

Clausing, Kimberly A. 2003. "Tax-Motivated Transfer Pricing and US Intrafirm Trade Prices." *Journal of Public Economics* 87: 2202–2223.

Cole, Adam J., Geoffrey Gee, and Nicholas Turner. 2011. "The Distributional and Revenue Consequences of Reforming the Mortgage Interest Deduction." *National Tax Journal* 64: 977–1000.

Congressional Budget Office. 2016. *The Distribution of Household Income and Federal Taxes, 2013.* https://www.cbo.gov/sites/default/files/114th-congress-2015-2016/reports/51361-householdincomefedtaxes.pdf.

Cronin, Julie Anne, Emily Y. Lin, Laura Power, and Michael Cooper. 2013. "Distributing the Corporate Income Tax: Revised U.S. Treasury Methodology." *National Tax Journal* 66: 239–262.

Democrats.org. 2016. *Our Platform.* https://www.democrats.org/party-platform \#fair -share.

Desai, M.A., C.F. Foley, and J.R. Hines, 2004. "Foreign Direct Investment in a World of Multiple Taxes." *Journal of Public Economics* 88: 2727–2744.

Dischinger, Matthias and Nadine Riedel. 2011. "Corporate taxes and the location of Intangible Assets within Multinational Firms." *Journal of Public Economics* 95: 691–707.

Dunsky, Robert M. and James R. Follain. 2000. "Tax-Induced Portfolio Reshuffling: The Case of the Mortgage Interest Deduction." *Real Estate Economics* 28: 683–718.

Edmiston, Kelly D. 2002. "Strategic Apportionment of the State Corporate Income Tax: An Applied General Equilibrium Analysis." *National Tax Journal* 60: 239–262.

Eichner, Thomas and Marco Runkel. 2008. "Why the European Union Should Adopt Formula Apportionment with a Sales Factor." *Scandinavian Journal of Economics* 110: 567–589.

Eng, Amanda. 2014. "Updated Options to Reform the Deduction for Home Mortgage Interest." The Urban Institute, May 7, 2014. http://www.urban.org/sites/default/files/publication/43116/413124-Updated-Options-to-Reform-the-Deduction-for-Home-Mortgage-Interest.PDF.

European Commission. 2001. *Towards an Internal Market without Tax Obstacles: A Strategy for Providing Companies with a Consolidated Corporate Tax Base for their EU-Wide Activities.* Brussels, Belgium: European Commission.

Follain, James R. and David C. Ling. 1991. "The Federal Tax Subsidy to Housing and the Reduced Value of the Mortgage Interest Deduction." *National Tax Journal* 44: 147–168.

Frank, Robert. 2011. "The Progressive Consumption Tax: A Win-Win Solution for Reducing American Income Inequality." *Slate*, December 7, 2011. http://www.slate.com/articles/business/moneybox/2011/12/the_progressive\consumption_tax_a_win_win_solution_for_reducing_american_economic_inequality_.html.

Frederick, Shane, George Loewenstein, and Ted O'Donoghue. 2002. "Time Discounting and Time Preference: A Critical Review." *Journal of Economic Literature* 40: 351–401.

Gale, William G., Jonathan Gruber, and Seth Stephens-Davidowitz. 2007. "Encouraging Homeownership Through the Tax Code." *Tax Notes* 115: 1171–1189.

Gentry, William M. and R. Glenn Hubbard. 1997. "Distributional Implications of Introducing a Broad-Based Consumption Tax." *Tax Policy and the Economy* 11: 1–47.

Gervais, Martin and Manish Pandey. 2008. "Who Cares about Mortgage Interest Deductibility?" *Canadian Public Policy* 34: 1–23.

Glaeser, Edward L., and Jesse Shapiro. 2003. "The Benefits of the Home Mortgage Interest Deduction." *Tax Policy and the Economy* 17: 37–82.

Goode, Richard. 1980. "The Superiority of the Income Tax." In Joseph A. Pechman, ed., *What Should Be Taxed: Income or Expenditure?* 49–73. Washington, DC: The Brookings Institute.

Graetz, Michael J. 1980. "Expenditure Tax Design." In Joseph A. Pechman, ed., *What Should Be Taxed: Income or Expenditure?* 161–295. Washington, DC: The Brookings Institute.

Graetz, Michael J. 1997. *The Decline (and Fall?) of the Income Tax.* New York, NY: W.W. Norton Co.

Graetz, Michael J. 2008. *100 Million Unnecessary Returns: A Simple, Fair, and Competitive Tax Plan for the United States.* New Haven CT: Yale University Press.

Gravelle, Jane G. 2001. "Whither Tax Depreciation?" *National Tax Journal* 54: 513–526.

Gravelle, Jane G. and Donald J. Marples. May 1, 2018. *Issues in International Corporate Taxation: The 2017 Revision (P.L. 115-97),* CRS Report R45186. Washington, DC: Library of Congress Congressional Research Service. https://fas.org/sgp/crs/misc/R45186.pdf.

Green, Richard K. and Kerry D. Vandell. 1999. "Giving Households Credit: How Changes in the U.S. Tax Code Could Promote Homeownership." *Regional Science and Urban Economics* 29: 419–444.

Griffith, Rachel, Helen Miller, and Martin O'Connell. 2014. "Ownership of Intellectual Property and Corporate Taxation." *Journal of Public Economics* 112: 12–23.

Grubert, Harry. 1998. "Taxes and the Division of Foreign Operating Income among Royalties, Interest, Dividends and Retained Earnings." *Journal of Public Economics* 68: 269–290.

Hall, Robert E. and Alvin Rabushka. 1995. *The Flat Tax.* 2nd ed. Stanford, CA: Hoover Institution Press.

Halperin, Daniel I. 1974. "Business Deduction for Personal Living Expenses: A Uniform Approach to an Unsolved Problem." *University of Pennsylvania Law Review* 122: 859–933.

Hanson, Andrew. 2012a. "A Better Tax System: The Progressive Consumption Tax." *MIC*, January 15, 2012. https://mic.com/articles/3352/a-better-tax-system-the-progressive-consumption-tax#.PADeApuXp.

Hanson, Andrew. 2012b. "The Incidence of the Mortgage Interest Deduction: Evidence from the Market for Home Purchase Loans." *Public Finance Review* 40: 339–359.

Hanson, Andrew. 2012c. "Size of Home, Homeownership, and the Mortgage Interest Deduction." *Journal of Housing Economics* 21: 195–210.

Harris, Benjamin H., C. Eugene Steuerle, and Amanda Eng. 2013. "New Perspectives on Homeownership Tax Incentives." *Tax Notes* 141: 1315–332.

Hilber, Christian A. L. and Tracy M. Turner. 2014. "The Mortgage Interest Deduction and Its Impact on Homeownership Decisions." *Review of Economics and Statistics* 96: 618–37.

Hines, James R. Jr. 2010. "Income Misattribution under Formula Apportionment." *European Economic Review* 54: 108–120.

Huizinga, Harry, Luc Laeven, and Gaetan Nicodeme. 2008. "Capital Structure and International Debt Shifting." *Journal of Financial Economics* 88: 80–118.

Institute for Fiscal Studies. 1978. *The Structure and Reform of Direct Taxation.* Report of a Committee Chaired by Professor J.E. Meade. London: Allen and Unwin.

Institute for Fiscal Studies. 2011. *Tax By Design: the Mirrlees Review.* New York, NY: Oxford University Press.

Kaldor, Nicholas. 1955. *An Expenditure Tax.* London: Allen and Irwin.

Kamin, David, David Gamage, Ari D. Glogower, Rebecca M. Kysar, Darien Shanske, Reuven S. Avi-Yonah, Lily L. Batchelder, J. Clifton Fleming, Daniel Jacob Hemel, Mitchell Kane, David S. Miller, Daniel Shaviro, and Manoj Viswanathan. 2017a. "The Games They Will Play: Tax Games, Roadblocks, and Glitches Under the New Legislation." December 7, 2017. http://dx.doi.org/10.2139/ssrn.3084187.

Kamin, David, David Gamage, Ari D. Glogower, Rebecca M. Kysar, Darien Shanske, Reuven S. Avi-Yonah, Lily L. Batchelder, J. Clifton Fleming, Daniel Jacob Hemel, Mitchell Kane, David S. Miller, Daniel Shaviro, and Manoj Viswanathan. 2017b. "The Games They Will Play: An Update on the Conference Committee Tax Bill." December 18, 2017. http://dx.doi.org/10.2139/ssrn.3089423.

Karkinsky, Tom and Nadine Riedel. 2012. "Corporate Taxation and the Choice of Patent Location within Multinational Firms." *Journal of Public Economics* 88: 176–185.

Keightley, Mark P. 2013. "An Analysis of Where American Companies Report Profits: Indications of Profit Shifting." *Congressional Research Service Report R42927*. Washington, DC: Library of Congress.

Keuschnigg, Christian and Mirela Keuschnigg. 2012. "Strategies in Enacting Fundamental Tax Reform." *National Tax Journal* 65: 357–385.

King, Mervyn. 1987. "The Cash-Flow Corporate Income Tax." In Martin Feldman, ed., *The Effects of Taxation on Capital Accumulation*, 377–398. Chicago: University of Chicago Press.

Kleinbard, Edward D. 2007. "Designing an Income Tax on Capital." In Henry J. Aaron, Leonard E. Burman, and C. Eugene Steuerle, eds., *Taxing Capital Income*, 165–210. Washington, DC: Urban Institute Press.

Maki, Dean M. 1996. "Portfolio Shuffling and Tax Reform." *National Tax Journal* 49: 317–329.

McCaffery, Edward J. 2005. "Good Hybrids/bad Hybrids." *Tax Notes:* 1699–1705.

McCaffery, Edward J. 2008. "A Consumed Income Tax: A Fair and Simple Plan for Tax Reform." http://dx.doi.org/10.2139/ssrn.1183583.

McGee, M. Kevin. 1989. "Alternative Transitions to a Consumption Tax." *National Tax Journal* 42: 155–166.

McGee, M. Kevin. 2017. "The Economic Distortions of a Border-Adjusted Corporate Cash Flow Tax." http://dx.doi.org/10.2139/ssrn.2944324.

Mieszkowski, Peter. 1978. "The Choice of Tax Base: Consumption versus Income Taxation." In *Federal Tax Reform: Myths and Realities*, 27–53. San Francisco, CA: Institute for Contemporary Studies.

Mieszkowski, Peter. 1980. "The Advisability and Feasibility of an Expenditure Tax System." In Henry J. Aaron and Michael J. Boskin, eds., *The Economics of Taxation*, 179–201. Washington, DC: The Brookings Institute.

Mills, L. and Newberry, K. 2004. "Do Foreign Multinationals' Tax Incentives Influence Their US Income Reporting and Debt Policy?" *National Tax Journal* 57: 89–107.

Minarek, Joseph J. 1985. *Making Tax Choices*. Washington, DC: The Urban Institute.

Moment of Truth. 2010. *Report of the National Commission on Fiscal Responsibility and Reform*. http://momentoftruthproject.org/report.

Musgrave, Richard A. 1976. "ET, OT, and SBT." *Journal of Public Economics* 6: 3–16.

New York Times. September 27, 2016. *Transcript of the First Debate*. https://www.ny times.com/2016/09/27/us/politics/transcript-debate.html.

OECD. 2007. *Fundamental Reform of Corporate Income Tax*. Paris: OECD Publishing. http://dx.doi.org/10.1787/9789264038127-en.

Poterba, James M. and Todd Sinai. 2008. "Tax Expenditures for Owner-Occupied Housing: Deductions for Property Taxes and Mortgage Interest and the Exclusion of Imputed Rental Income." *American Economic Review* 98: 84–89.

President's Advisory Panel on Federal Tax Reform. 2005. *Simple, Fair, and Pro–Growth: Proposals to Fix America's Tax System*. Washington, DC: U.S. Government Printing Office.

Republican Platform. 2016. *Restoring the American Dream*. https://www.gop.com/platform/restoring-the-american-dream/.

Rosen, Harvey S. and Ted Gayer. 2010. *Public Finance*. 9th ed. New York, NY: McGraw-Hill.

Rosenthal, Steven M. 2017. "Slashing Corporate Taxes: Foreign Investors Are Surprise Winners." *Tax Notes* 157: p. 559.

Saez, Emmanual and Gabriel Zucman. 2015. "Wealth Inequality in the United States since 1913; Evidence from Capitalized Income Tax Data." http://eml.berkeley.edu/~saez.

Saez, Emmanual and Gabriel Zucman. 2016. "Wealth Inequality in the United States since 1913; Evidence from Capitalized Income Tax Data." *Quarterly Journal of Economics* 131: 519–578.

Sarkar, Shounak and George R. Zodrow. 1993. "Transitional Issue in Moving to a Direct Consumption Tax." *National Tax Journal* 46: 359–376.

Seidman, Laurence S. 1984. "Conversion to a Consumption Tax: The Transition in a Life-Cycle Growth Model" *Journal of Political Economy* 92: 211–267.

Seidman, Laurence S. 1997. *The USA Tax: A Progressive Consumption Tax*. Cambridge MA: MIT Press.

Seidman, Laurence S. 2009. *Public Finance*. New York, NY: McGraw-Hill.

Shoven, John B. 1978. "Inflation and Income Taxation." In *Federal Tax Reform: Myths and Realities*, 171–188. San Francisco CA: Institute for Contemporary Studies.

Simons, Henry C. 1938. *Personal Income Taxation: The Definition of Income as a Problem of Fiscal Policy*. Chicago IL: University of Chicago Press.

Skinner, Jonathan and Daniel Feenberg. 1990. "Impact of the 1986 Tax Reform on Personal Saving." In Joel Slemrod, ed. *Do Taxes Matter?: The Impact of the Tax Reform Act of 1986*, Cambridge, MA: Massachusetts Institute of Technology.

Steuerle, C. Eugene. 2003. "The Latest 'ZITCOM' and My New Tax Shelter Bank." *Tax Notes* 99: 739–740.

Steuerle, C. Eugene. 2004. *Contemporary U.S. Tax Policy*. Washington, DC: The Urban Institute.

Stiglitz, Joseph E. 1985. "The Consumption-Expenditure Tax." In Joseph A. Pechman, ed., *The Promise of Tax Reform*. 107–127. Englewood Cliffs, NJ: Prentice-Hall.

Stiglitz, Joseph E. 2000. *Economics of the Public Sector,* 3rd ed. New York, NY: W.W. Norton.

Summers, Lawrence H. 1981. "Capital Taxation and Accumulation in a Life Cycle Growth Model." *American Economic Review* 74: 533–544.

Tax Policy Center. September 16, 2016. "House GOP Tax Plan: Impact on Revenue 2016–2026 by Fiscal Year and Total for FY2027-36." http://www.taxpolicycenter .org/model-estimates/house-gop-tax-plan-sep-2016/t16-0208-house-gop-tax-plan -impact-tax-revenue-2016-26.

Thaler, Richard H. 1999. "Mental Accounting Matters." *Behavioral Decision Making* 12: 183–206.

Thaler, Richard H. and Cass R. Sunstein. 2008. *Nudge*. New Haven: Yale University Press.

U.S. Small Business Administration. 2018. *Firm Size Data*. https://www.sba.gov/ advocacy/firm-size-data.

U.S. Treasury Department. October 16, 2017. *Tax Expenditures*. https://www.treasury .gov/resource-center/tax-policy/Documents/Tax-Expenditures-FY2019.pdf.

Viard, Alan D. 2014. "Move to a Progressive Consumption Tax." *Cato Online Forum*, November 18, 2014. https://www.cato.org/conference-forum/reviving-economic -growth.

Weisbach, David A. 2006. "The Case for a Consumption Tax." *Tax Notes* 110: 1357–1359.

Wolff, Edward N. 2017. "Deconstructing Household Wealth Trends in the United States, 1983 to 2016." November 27, 2017. wid.world/wp-content/uploads/2017/11/020 -Wolff.pdf.

Yglesias, Matthew. 2010. "Progressive Consumption Taxes." *Think Progress*, August 7, 2010. https://thinkprogress.org/progressive-consumption-taxes-fb5ae8d2ef0e.

Zodrow, George. 1991. "On the 'Traditional' and 'New' Views of Dividend Taxation." *National Tax Journal* 44: 497–509.

Zucman, Gabriel. 2014. "Taxing across Borders: Tracking Personal Wealth and Corporate Profits." *Journal of Economic Perspectives* 28: 121–148.

Index

About the Author

M. Kevin McGee is professor emeritus in economics at the University of Wisconsin Oshkosh, where he taught public sector economics for 33 years. His research interests vary widely; he has published articles on a variety of topics, including tax policy, decision making under risk, and the measurement of competitive balance.